I0620950

The Musical Gift

Music Theory for Everyone

By Michael Preussner

Volume One- How To Think About Music

Thanks

These wonderful folks were instrumental in the creating of this book:

To Keith Barefoot, Kraig Grady, Martha Ronk, Timothy Emmons, and Adam Nimoy.
Couldn't have done it without you.
To all of the amazing musicians I grew up with and have been inspired by.
To my L.A. pals and fellow drummers- Ralph Penland and Sonship Theus.
To Craig Woodson, Billy Moore, James Wing Woo, and Dorrance Stalvey.
Thank you for all that you taught me.
To Dr. Ron Carter, for opening my mind and ears.
To my grandmother FrauDr. Hildegard Preussner and uncles George Leasim and Stuart O'Brien.

To the city of Portland, Oregon for making many things possible.
To George Colligan, who extended a real helping hand when I needed it.

And many thanks to all of the students I have had the pleasure of teaching and learning from.

The Musical Gift- Volume One   Copyright © 2025 Michael Preussner   All Rights Reserved

Dedication

This book is dedicated to the members of the Tony Williams Quintet.
To Wallace Roney, Bill Pierce, Charnett Moffett, Ira Coleman, Mulgrew Miller, Tony Williams,
and also Lee Ethier

Thank you for all you generously gave me, which continues to inspire me to this day.

Introduction

The intention behind this book started with a simple idea- to present the musical universe in a way that could be understood by everyone. This idea developed and morphed over time as I taught piano lessons to every imaginable kind of student- all styles, levels, and ages. Eventually a piano system emerged that seemed to teach virtually anyone. Practically every lesson I would find myself exploring some musical concept using a new way to think about it for a particular student. Layer upon layer from many different angles over the years. My college friend Steve Elder once said this to me when I asked him why he taught guitar. He smiled and answered, "It's the best way to learn". He was right.

Quite a while passed between that initial idea and an actual book materializing. It seemed that nearly every time I spoke to someone about it, it would change. Especially when talking with those that had studied music seriously but then had stopped somewhere along the way because it had become too difficult for one reason or another. Some good players felt they weren't 'good enough'. One thing I kept hearing was the desire to learn more about music and to continue participating in the musical world as both a player and listener. They loved it. But somehow their progress had been halted or thwarted by persistent negative beliefs. A sad tale I heard many times.

I heard people say things like they were fundamentally unable to move beyond a certain point because they didn't have the talent or ability to go further. Many held the belief that the great musicians they admired were in possession of some kind of magical ability that few have. Certainly true for some of the greats, but every one of the greats became great by working at it. That makes the biggest difference, to never give up.

I spoke to folks that had studied music but then had stopped playing completely. They still held a desire to get back into it but felt it was too much and they couldn't devote enough time to solve all of the problems that had kept them stuck. Many felt the mysteries were too deep and the gray areas too vast and had all but given up hope of ever getting deeper into it, as if they had waited too long and all was lost. I wanted to hand them a book and say, "Here, just do this".

I wanted to show all of them that they usually knew a lot more than they thought and only needed a few parts of the puzzle cleared up. Also that it's okay to stop if you get confused or overwhelmed. That's what is so wonderful about music. Even when you don't play the mind still works at it, so it's very common to not practice for a long time and come back sounding better. As if you were practicing the whole time. You were.

I have always wanted to show people that they are wrong when they tear themselves down like that. Wrong about this imagined infinite distance between themselves and the musical world. There is a better way to understand our modern musical system. They should keep searching. There is always a way. Music is a human friendly system and is such a magnificent use of our collective experiences. A universal language without any of the usual barriers. Music can convey an amazing variety of emotions and be extremely satisfying to listen to. I believe it makes us smarter. I'm not alone in that belief.

Dr Oliver Sachs wrote a great book titled **Musicophilia** about all of the unique ways the neural pathways and synapses work within our brains when stimulated by music. It seems our minds are fired up by music in ways that are at a level virtually unmatched by most other brain functions. A lot of brain power is activated.

Music classes were always in schools back in my day. And all of the smart kids were in them, all the math geniuses. Why? Because the organization within music stimulates the brain and is very pleasing when it all works out, as it did in most of the classical repertoire we played. Students would be working their brains but in a different, less academic way. The activity is fun so the mathematics were invisible. There also was a wonderful cultural and social aspect within the uplifting experiences of these students playing together in ensembles. A whole different part of their education. And these experiences were shared by everyone.

Music is everyone's birthright. Yes, you too, dear reader. Music is for everyone. It is our Musical Gift.

That is how this book idea evolved and became focused on a very practical goal. After a long time teaching privately I found myself working with college students that wanted to fill in any gaps they felt they had in their musical knowledge. What had begun as a basic piano course for all styles, levels, and ages now included a streamlined college level prep course in music theory that could help a new student hit their first year running. No matter which way they went within the curriculum they would be prepared, perhaps even over prepared, with all the necessary skills. A student would be able to then take full advantage of the complete resources at their school from the very first day in class. Good for everyone all around, hopefully helping in the process of some great music being created by new players out in the world. We all win.

A few words about myself.
I formally studied 4 different music theory systems in college while obsessed with the piano music of Bela Bartok. The first theory book was by Walter Piston, then came Robert Ottman, then Vincent Persichetti (a great book called Twentieth Century Harmony). Finishing with Arnold Schoenberg and his tonal regional analysis in classes with my mentor Dorrance Stalvey, himself a great composer and musical genius. And many other things. Dorrance ran the Monday Evening Concert series at the L.A. County Art Museum for many years. After he passed away I learned at one time he was Stravinsky's copyist. He never told me that.

In Dorrance's analysis class I would analyze Brahms Intermezzi off the page, but none of it made much sense in practical terms. It was like math, and even after all that study it just wasn't of much use in reality. I knew the harmony abstractly but didn't really connect it to the sounds and functions within that harmony.

After many years of playing jazz professionally as a drummer, I decided to study jazz piano. I wanted to learn how 'jazz theory' is actually used out in the real world and discovered it's really the same thing and that modern jazz theory is also very practical. There is no difference as far as style. The same ideas and principles apply for classical, jazz, folk, rock, really all music. The structural and architectural theory behind the sounds is the same. Harmony is based on physics, known as 'acoustic law'. Consonance and dissonance are physical manifestations of sound moving through air.

There just hasn't been a basic music theory book, a shop manual if you will, for *everyone*. Until now.
This is the theory book I wish I'd had when I was studying, using the piano keyboard as a sort of master control panel for conceptualizing the whole thing. All the great composers were piano players for a reason.

I designed this book with a very big nod to the original "idiot book" for Volkwagens by the late John Muir. His book was a repair manual filled with fabulous anecdotes and wonderful advice that provided much more than a resource for learning how to be self sufficient and work on your own car. Many times his observations applied to life itself. This made the actual work easier and deeper at the same time, stimulating the real sign of intelligence- curiosity. Full of homespun wisdom, perfect for self starters. Now at last I can present such a book to you. Not just for college students, but for everyone.

You are encouraged to read these chapters as far as you can even if it seems to push you into uncharted territory. Also feel free to skip ahead or around jumping from chapter to chapter. To use an analogy, if it doesn't make sense reading the night before you do that engine job, it will tomorrow morning when you are under the car. This book attempts to bypass a lot of the overly technical confusion and go directly to playing. It is designed so that each lesson is short, often just a page or two. It is advised that you read the lesson first even if it doesn't all make sense. It will when you play it, even if you play it one note at a time slowly. Don't be afraid to push ahead into the unknown. We're all in this together.
I hope you enjoy exploring your *Musical Gift*.

The Musical Gift

Volume One- How To Think About Music

Table of Contents

The Musical Gift

How To Use This Book

It is my belief that the entire musical system is friendly to the way we think. That the patterns imbedded in our musical world are the same patterns that we use deeply in our brains.

In this study we will use the piano keyboard to access this natural ability we all share. Although the intention behind the creating of this book is how to think about music, here we will use our bodies. We will use and develop the synaptic connections in our brain through the coordinated movements of our fingers. These motions will naturally develop the complex neural pathways that exist when playing music at the piano, the best instrument for thinking of our musical system.

Our goal is to reach the unconscious mind somatically and then tap into the programming that is already there. And once you build a strong foundation there you can go on to anywhere your imagination takes you. This knowledge applies to any instrument and all styles of music.

It may seem like a contradiction to do this. There is a lot to understand and one can get confused along the way. The good news is solving problems is fun for the mind, so let it work naturally. The organization has already been done for you here in this book. All one has to do is play as instructed through each lesson until it is understood. Generally follow the sequence but feel free to skip around. Each lesson is intentionally short, so one can go little by little, one page at a time. There is no rush. When you can play the lesson and feel you know it proceed to the next one. You have full control over your progress.

The idea of a 'hands on' approach to learn how to think may be a difficult paradox to grasp. Get used to it. Many paradoxes exist in this subject and throughout this book. Here's just one example.

We will intensely learn just one key completely to then understand all twelve keys. The structure is the same but otherwise the twelve keys are all different and unique. They all sound different, and on the piano they all look and feel different. The twelve keys are the same, but different. These kinds of paradoxes can stretch our conventional thinking. A good place to start.

Trust the process. Proceed fearlessly. Here at last is music 'theory' presented simply and clearly. Our musical inheritance. It belongs to all of us. We are already members in this club.

Welcome to your Musical Gift.

The Piano Keyboard

The **piano keyboard**. Think of it like a master control panel for our entire musical system. All the great composers were excellent piano players. One could point to the music of J.S. Bach or Duke Ellington as examples of writing for ensembles that really sound like an extension of the keyboard. Sometimes listening one can imagine a giant keyboard.
The one we use now has a long history and evolved over that time.
With basic keyboard skills one has access to a huge potential and a vast tradition.

The piano keyboard has many advantages for a number of reasons that will be very clear almost instantly. It is unsurpassed for conceiving music, although all instruments certainly have their own advantages. We will use it as the main instrument in this study, but all of this knowledge easily transfers to other instruments. This is formally known as **Orchestration**. The music of the great Maurice Ravel is a brilliant example of this skill. He was able to write a beautiful piece for piano solo and then later orchestrate it just as beautifully. Ravel is unmatched in this skill and has been studied by many modern arrangers like Gil Evans.

Let's jump right in and have a look at the keyboard. The first thing to notice is the keys are black and white. Sometimes the piano is referred to as the 'black and whites'. See the two different groupings of black keys. There are 2 black keys, then 3 black keys, in a repeating pattern up and down the keyboard. How many times this pattern repeats depends on the size of your keyboard.

The piano or a full sized keyboard has 88 keys. Our first advantage. 88 notes is a lot. Some keyboards are smaller but the idea is the same. Many instruments have only one note. Members of the string family typically have 4 notes. The guitar has 6 notes.

The important thing here is to identify the two groups of black keys and then just the group of 2 black keys. Play the white key just below any group of 2 black keys. This is our first note, C.

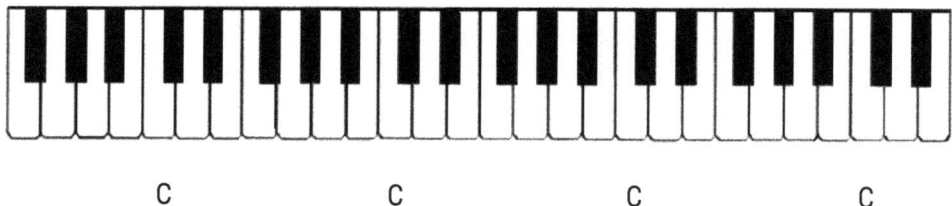

If you end up playing the note below the group of 3 black keys, this is the note F.

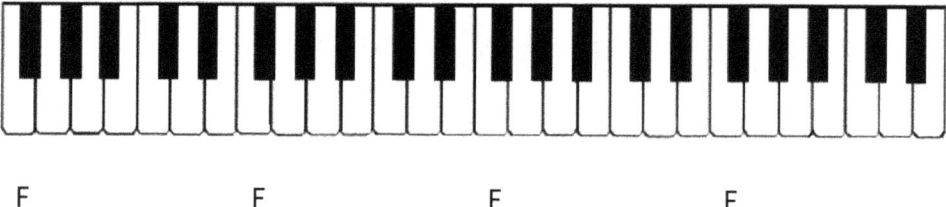

Middle C and The C Major Scale

Although there are differing schools of thought on where to start and why, in this case we will start with C as our first 'locater'. See how many C's you have on your keyboard. Count them. If you have a full sized 88 key keyboard there are a total of 8 C's. Find the C note in the middle of the keyboard. This is called **Middle C**.

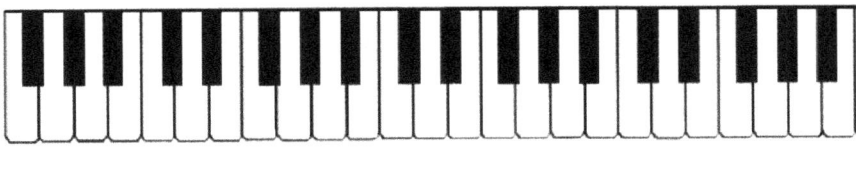

Middle C

The C Major Scale

The Musical Alphabet

Many great musicians and music teachers believe that starting with the **C major scale** is too hard or wrong. It's said that Chopin started his students in the key of B major, which is a great key on the piano keyboard. It's hard to argue with any case made about the difficulty of the C scale on the piano keyboard since it is all white keys. It's very easy to get lost as you move quickly, like being snow blind. Your fingers have to be positioned perfectly and the right distance apart when playing chords quickly, for example. But here we'll use C and learn it really well, and then use all of that knowledge for the other keys. There are good reasons for this. For example, altering notes in the scale- known as **accidentals**- can be seen visually in C and then easily **transposed** to any other key.

The **musical alphabet** has seven letters- A, B, C, D, E, F, and G. These repeat up and down seven tones using the white keys. Start with any finger and play up and down from any C to the next C. One **octave** of the **C major scale**. Say or sing the alphabet while playing forwards and backwards. Especially backwards since we have less practice that way. Yes, music moves in both directions. The familiar do re mi etc. are the syllables for the scale in an Italian musical language- **solfeggio**.

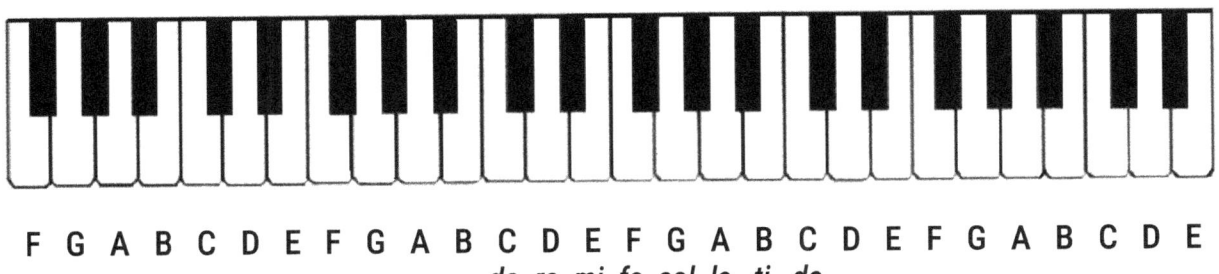

F G A B C D E F G A B C D E F G A B C D E F G A B C D E
do re mi fa sol la ti do

Music Notation and The Great Staff

The Answer Page

Music is written down as **Musical Notation.** Notes are written down on the page and the pitches are positioned on the **Great or Grand Staff**. You may not believe it yet, but this page has many of the answers you will need for this book- all in one place. You might think of this as the **Answer Page.**

Knowing the **Great Staff** allows us to visually access a great deal of information quickly. Just by looking at a page of music we can mentally process a lot before we even play a note.

Middle C divides the upper and lower ranges of the great staff. The right hand mostly plays the notes above middle C, the left hand mostly plays the notes below middle C. Sometimes the hands really move around or even cross over each other, but this is generally the case. Let's take a look at **2 octaves** of the C major scale on the keys and the staff together.

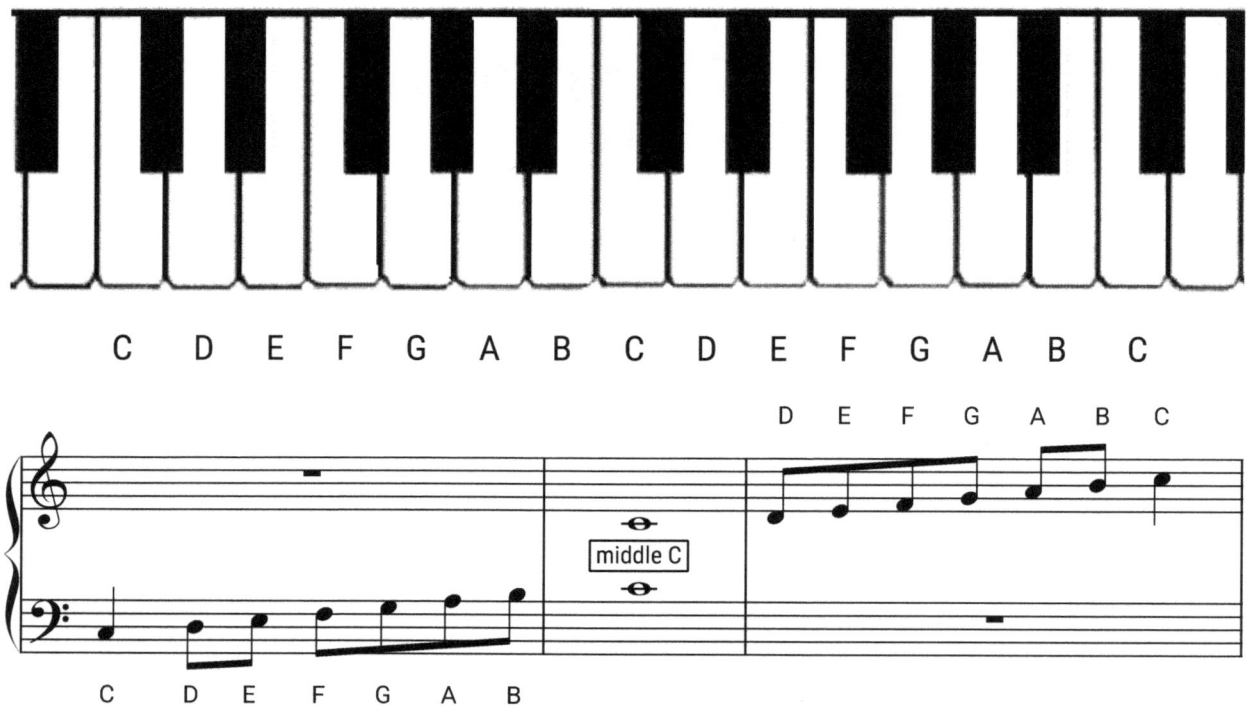

Here are **4 octaves** of the C scale. There are tricks to help you learn the staff on the next 2 pages.

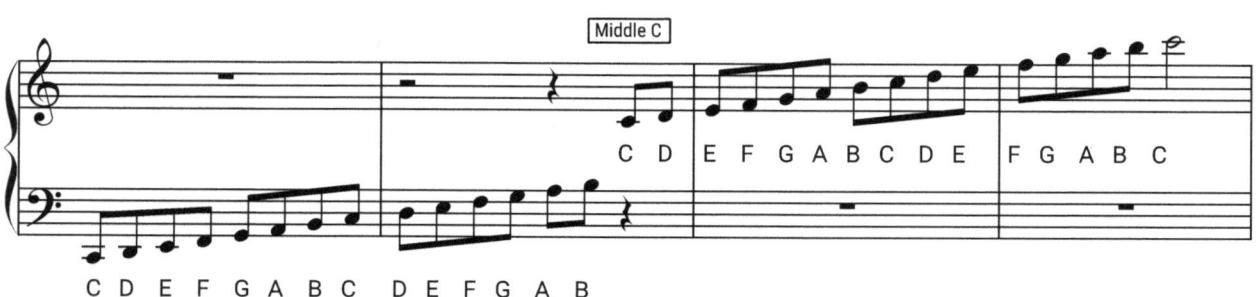

The Treble Clef

The G Clef

The **_Treble Clef_** shows us the notes in the **higher register above middle C**. The treble clef symbol evolved from a fancy letter G. With a little imagination we can see that the scroll of the G starts on the inside and circles the G line. It is saying "here is G".

G line

The Bass Clef

The F Clef

The **_Bass Clef_** shows us the notes in the **lower register below middle C**. The bass clef symbol evolved from a fancy letter F. With a little imagination we can see that the scroll at the beginning of the F starts on the F line and the two dots are above and below it. It is saying "here is F".

F line

Reading the Great Staff

The Great Staff arranges notes on *lines and spaces*. Movements of notes up and down on the page match the up and down movements in pitches. Here are some tricks to help you read the notes. Notation is traditionally taught starting in the treble clef.

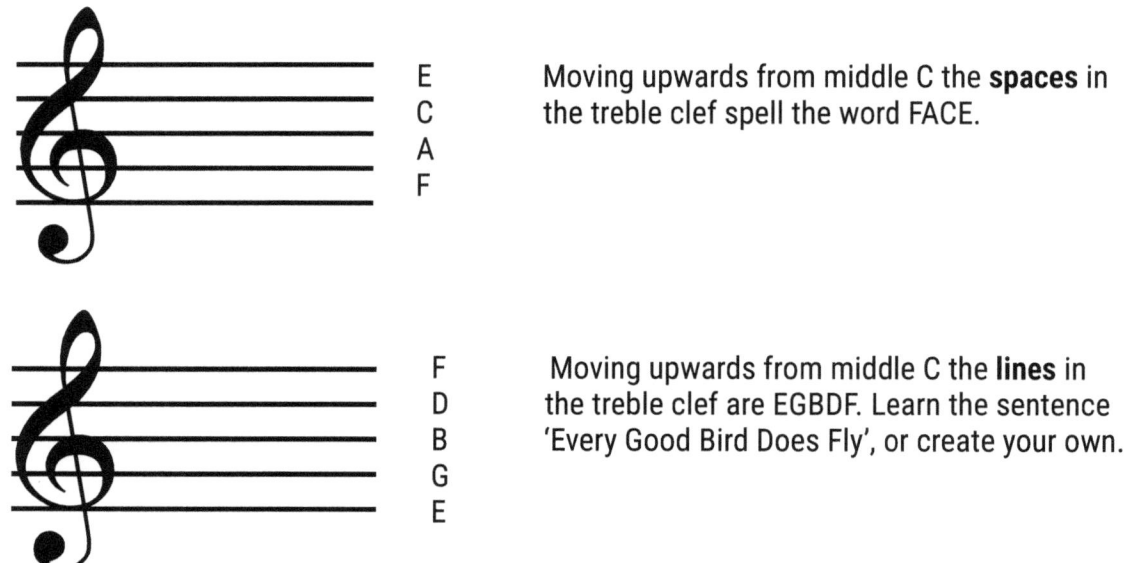

E
C
A
F

Moving upwards from middle C the **spaces** in the treble clef spell the word FACE.

F
D
B
G
E

Moving upwards from middle C the **lines** in the treble clef are EGBDF. Learn the sentence 'Every Good Bird Does Fly', or create your own.

We can really learn the notes on the staff quickly using *intervals*. Intervals are explained in more detail in Chapter 2. Here we'll use the idea of **mirroring** the same exact intervals up or down from middle C. We'll first use the interval of an *octave*. Play these notes **with** middle C on the keyboard. Play the next C **up** an octave from middle C- on the **second** space from the **top** of the treble clef. Then play C **down** an octave from middle C- on the **second** space from the **bottom** of the bass clef. Moving *up* another octave above the treble clef the next higher C has **2 ledger lines**. Play it. Moving *down* another octave below the bass clef the next lower C also has **2 ledger lines**. Play it. Play G above middle C and F below it. More mirroring. This time using a new interval of a *5th*. G is *up a 5th* on the second line up from middle C. Like a mirror F is *down a 5th* on the second line down from middle C. Here are all these helpful intervals shown together mirroring from middle C.

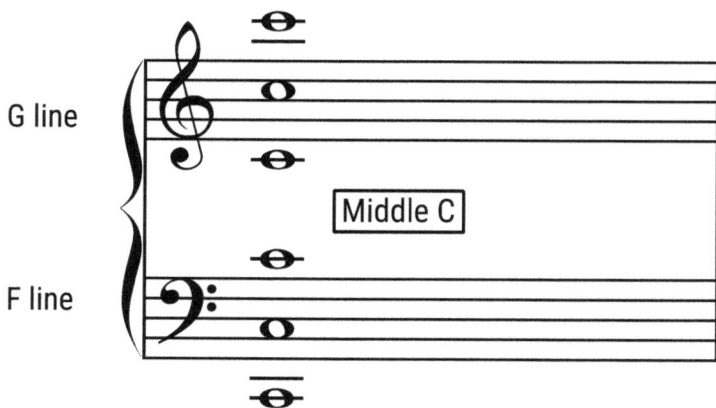

G line

F line

Middle C

Fingering for The Hands

The Right hand and Left hand work in a mirror like way when we do simple everyday tasks. For example, try drinking a glass of water from each hand. See how they reflect each other doing this.

Put your finger tips together. Touch the thumbs to each other. This is finger number **1** in each hand.

Touch each finger in the Right hand to it's opposite finger in the Left hand **one at a time**. Do this from the thumb to the little finger back and forth several times.

We have 5 fingers in each hand. We number them 1 through 5 starting at the thumb and moving to the little finger. Now lay your hands flat next to each other in front of you. See the mirroring?

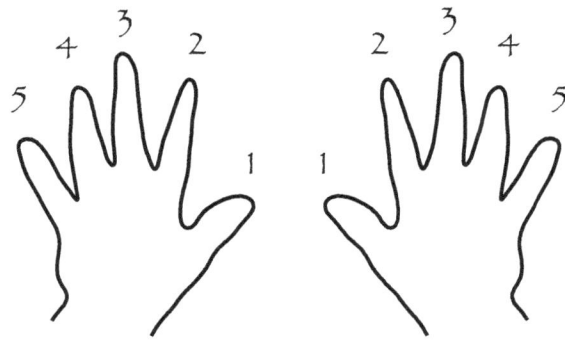

5 Finger Position in C Major~ Right Hand

Place the right hand **only** on the keyboard with the thumb on middle C. This is called **5 finger C position** or just **C position** at middle C. There is more than one C position on your keyboard. Let each of your 5 fingers feel each of the 5 white keys in middle C position. Play them one at a time and listen. Mentally picture these 5 notes on the staff- C, D, E, F, and G.

Right hand fingering:

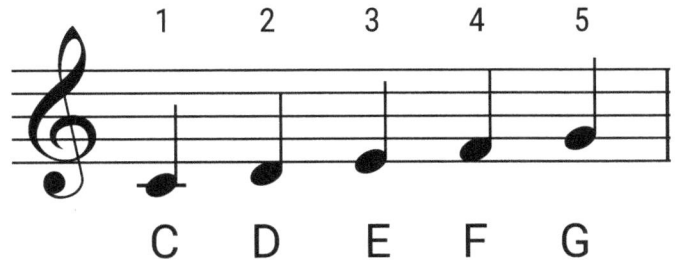

The Note Pyramid

or The Rhythm Pyramid

Note Type		Count

Whole Note

Whole measure
(4 counts in 4/4)

1   2   3   4

Half Note

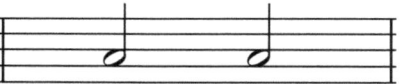

2 counts

1 2 / 3 4

Quarter Note

1 count

1 / 2 / 3 / 4

Eighth Note

Half count

1 and / 2 and / 3 and / 4 and

Keeping Time- Measures and Bar Lines
Using The Note Pyramid

Now **play** the note pyramid while counting time. We will count using what is called ***common time***. Common time, also known as 4/4, means we count in groups of 4 beats within a ***measure***.
In common time count 4 quarter notes per measure that each get 1 count. **Rest** means don't play.
Measures are divided by ***bar lines***, usually just called ***bars***. Many songs are grouped in ***systems*** of measures. Have you heard of a 12 bar blues? It means the song is 12 measures long.

4 bar system- rests

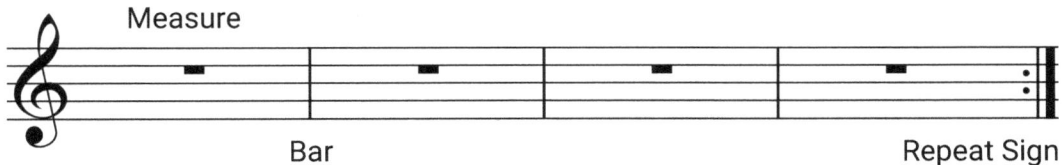

Try to **count out loud** while you play the notes in order starting from the top of the note pyramid. Each measure has **twice** the number of notes as the previous measure, played **twice** as fast. Count evenly 1, 2, 3, 4. Hold longer notes for their full time value or ***duration***. Start slowly. Repeat this as directed by the ***repeat sign***. Play on middle C or note of your choice.

4 bar system- Note/Rhythm pyramid

Count evenly in 4 playing each note as written. Hold notes for their full duration.

Now we'll try playing some familiar songs in common time. We'll start with the right hand playing in ***5 finger middle C position***. Play these in the right hand only and make sure to count out loud evenly 1,2,3,4 as you play. Play slowly at first.

Songs in 5 Finger C Position

Let's try playing some songs. Play what you see on the staff. First just play the notes in order as you would normally read- from left to right. Then try counting *in time* while you play.
Count 1,2,3,4. See if you can recognize the songs. Here we will start using *finger numbers*.

Right hand C position

Now we will get rid of the unnecessary visual clutter. Fingerings are shown only when needed

Right hand

Time Signatures
Counting in Time

Time signatures tell us two things. **How many**? And **what** are we counting?

The top number of the time signature shows
us **How Many** counts per *measure*.
Here it says 4 counts per measure.

The bottom number tells us **What** we are
counting. Think of it like a fraction.
One over four or 1/4 is one fourth, or one Quarter.
So we count 4 quarter notes per *measure*.

4/4 is by far the most common time signature. The symbol C stands for common time.
The symbol 4/4 and the symbol C are interchangeable.

Here are some other time signatures we will further explain and use in later chapters.

Rests

It is very important to know when to play and when **not** to play. *Rests* are symbols for silence.

There are symbols for the various rests just like for the notes. We can think of rests in the same order using the Rhythm pyramid on page 8 and count them the same way- but don't play, just count.

Whole rests take up the whole measure regardless of the time signature. See the example in 3/4.

Whole rest in 3/4

Although whole and half note rests look the same, they are different Look closely. Whole rests **hang** from the bar line because they're 'heavier'.

As we continue into the next chapter the first thing we'll look at are the common scales that are used in music. These will become your basic vocabulary and a great source for many other scales.

Each lesson is intentionally short, usually a page or two, and explains a complete concept. Feel free to experiment with each idea after playing and understanding it. Try moving to different places on the keyboard, for example, and listen to the changes. Fingering is specific only where shown. Otherwise try some different fingers to see which are better for you. Let your imagination take you where it wants to go. Be creative. Fingering will naturally evolve and move towards consistency.

In later chapters there will be much more specific instructions for fingering that should be followed exactly and the reasons for these will be shown as we move forward.

Thinking About Scales- The 4 Basic Scales

Behind the pleasing experience of listening to music lies structure. The skillful musician has a broad knowledge of the basic architecture and principles of *Harmony*. Notes that sound pleasing to us are actually based on physics. The movement of sound through the air follows *Acoustic Law*. Later we will see how our musical system uses the organization within the *Overtone Series*.

Our modern system has evolved into a complex musical canvas that is based on three elements. *Harmony*, *Melody*, and *Rhythm*. Music exists in **time**. Harmony and melody are driven by rhythm.

Harmony and *Melody* can actually be understood as the same thing. One good way to picture this conceptually is by thinking of horizontal harmony (melody) and vertical harmony (chords) as one might play or sing music, or how one sees it on the written page when reading musical *Notation*.

The *Scales* are like the pools of organized notes we draw from to make most of our melodies and harmonies. There are *4 common types of scales* that use selected notes from the *Chromatic Scale*. These 4 basic types are the *Major*, *Minor*, *Whole Tone*, and *Diminished* scales. Let's have a look.

The **1st scale type** is the *Major* scale. There are 7 notes in this scale. There are 12 major scales. The **2nd scale type** is the *Minor* scale. There are 7 notes in this scale. There are 12 minor scales. There are several different variations of the minor scale as we will see.

A major **or** minor scale can be built starting on each of the 12 notes of the chromatic scale. Structurally **all** of the different **minor** scales can be understood as **variants of the major scale**.

The **3rd scale type** is the *Whole Tone* scale. There are 6 notes in this scale. There are 2 of these.

The **4th scale type** is the *Diminished* scale. There are 8 notes in this scale. There are 3 of these.

So our study begins with learning **all 12** major, **12** minor, **2** whole tone, and **3** diminished scales.

These are the basic building blocks of our musical system. Of course there are many different scales from all over the world. These differences will be much clearer after learning the basics.

To learn all of these scales might seem like an impossible task at first if you are just starting out on your musical journey. Or perhaps you are already an experienced musician but find all of this confusing or even overwhelming. I have encountered many frustrated students caught in this bind.

There are ways to understand scales that make it much easier than it might first appear. We will start just with the **structure of the major scale**. It is the same structure for all 12 of these scales. By learning this structure really well in one key, in this case C major, we can then understand all 12 major scales as the same basic idea instead of trying to learn 12 completely different things.

As we start looking closer at our first major scale, C major, you will see right away that these complexities are made especially easy for us to comprehend as we play on the piano keyboard.

The Chromatic Scale

It's best to start with all the notes. The *Chromatic Scale* uses **all 12 notes** within one **octave**. It is also known as the **half step** scale since it is made up entirely of musical half steps. The half step is the smallest *scale degree* moving from any note to the next nearest note. Two half steps together make a **whole step (or whole tone)**.

The word *Chroma* in ancient Greek loosely translates as "color" or "all colors".

We'll add the 5 black keys to the 7 white keys of the C major scale for a total of 12 notes on the keyboard. If you don't know them, they are now your new friends. Here we start with every note.

Play the chromatic scale in the Right Hand and Left Hand **separately** and make sure to keep the hands relaxed. This is an excellent way to train the hands to naturally stay aligned towards the keys without any awkward motions. Start slowly and then work up to a faster *tempo*. Always stay relaxed. Pay close attention to keeping the fingerings exactly as shown.

Look carefully at this pattern on the keyboard.

2 white key pattern:

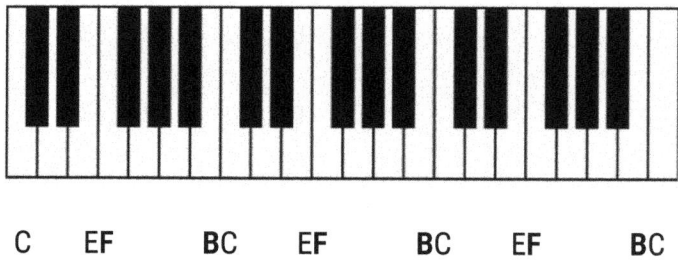

C   EF   BC   EF   BC   EF   BC

Fingering for the Chromatic scale:

Use the **3rd finger** on **all the black keys.** Use the 2nd finger **only** when there are two white keys right next to each other. This happens **twice** per octave- between E and F and again between B and C. It turns out that F and B is the *tritone interval* of the C scale- more about tritone intervals later.

The Chromatic Scale- Hands Separately

We'll begin by playing the chromatic scale one hand at a time starting with the right hand only.
Make sure to **follow the fingering exactly** to properly align each hand at the keyboard.
Play an octave of the chromatic scale **ascending and descending** reading the *treble clef*.
Refer to the Great Staff (Answer Page) to learn any note names. We're learning some new things.
Accidental signs change the note and stay in effect until the end of the measure.
The *sharp* sign (#) **raises** a note by one half step. Here sharps are shown when *ascending*.
The *flat* sign (b) **lowers** a note by one half step. Here flats are shown when *descending*.
Use the **3rd finger on all black keys**. The **2nd** finger is used only **twice** per octave as shown.

Right hand only- carefully watch fingering.

Then play an octave *descending* and *ascending* in the left hand reading the notes in the *bass clef*.
Again the **3rd finger** is on all **black keys**, the **2nd finger** is used only **twice** per octave as shown.
Refer to the Great Staff (Answer Page) as needed to learn any note names.

Left hand only- carefully watch fingering.

In measure 3 we learn another new sign, the *natural* sign. This sign **cancels** out any accidentals.

When this feels comfortable play **two or more octaves** first with the right hand only **ascending and descending** and then the left hand only **descending and ascending** starting from middle C.

The Tetrachord
How To Build A Scale From Any Note

The **Tetrachord** is a pattern within the major scale. It is whole step, whole step, half step.

It occurs *twice* in the scale and can be thought of as two identical 4 note chords. Tetrachords are built using the intervals of 2 whole steps and then a half step. Playing them is a good way to feel the actual contour of a key. The **first tetrachord** in the C major scale would be the notes C D E and F.

Play these notes in your left hand using the fingers 4321. Play them separately and then together.

Skip a whole step and build the **second tetrachord** in your right hand using 1234, placed directly above the left hand. Whole, whole, half step for the notes G A B and C. Play these in your right hand. The thumbs of both hands are next to each other with the 4th finger of each hand playing C.

Now you have built the C major scale starting and ending on C using 2 tetrachords.
Let's try building another scale. Remember the tetrachord pattern.
Whole, whole, half **left,** then *skip a whole step*, then whole, whole, half **right**.

Pick any note. Let's pick F for this example. The first tetrachord is on F G A and Bb in the left hand. Skip a whole step and build the second tetrachord on the notes C D E and F in the right hand.

As you see, the F major scale has one flat. That is unique. F is the only major scale with one flat.

Major Scales and Fingering

When playing the piano it is obvious that the C scale is fairly easy to understand. It's almost as if the keyboard has been set up especially for C. Once you can recognize where C is you can build a major scale from there. But almost right away you can come up against some new challenges. The first one as already mentioned is that it is all white keys and that can be confusing. But the hard thing to work out is how to play a scale smoothly in one hand? How? With fingering.

A major scale is 7 different tones. If you want to play an octave of the complete C scale up and down it would include another C. An eighth tone. So think of the major scale as 7+1= 8. Seven different tones starting at the root and then again playing the root at the top. Since we have only 5 fingers to play these 8 notes we can use *fingering*. We'll start with playing one octave of the scale.

7 equals 3 + 4 **or** 4 + 3. So play 7 notes with 2 groups of fingers. Use 3 fingers, then 4. Play the 8th tone with the 5th finger. The first 3 fingers are used twice and the **4th finger** is only used **once** per *octave*. Play in the right hand using the **4th finger only** on the **B**. Also watch the thumb moving to F. Although many learn it as 'thumb under' it's better to move the entire hand to *F position* if you can.

Now play the right hand two octaves up and down. When descending and you run out of fingers ask yourself- is the next note a B or an E? If it's a B, use your 4th finger. If it's an E use your 3rd finger.

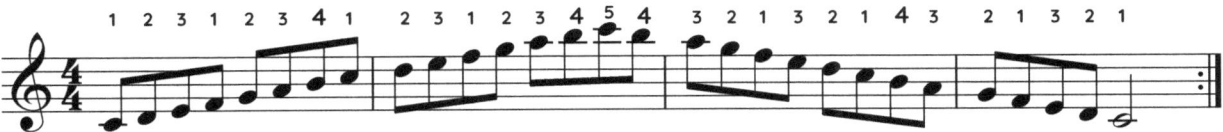

Let's do something here that lets the right hand 'teach' the left hand the fingering using mirroring. Start with **both** thumbs on middle C and move both hands in opposite directions. As the hands mirror each other, the thumbs always **move at the same time** as they go away and come back to C.

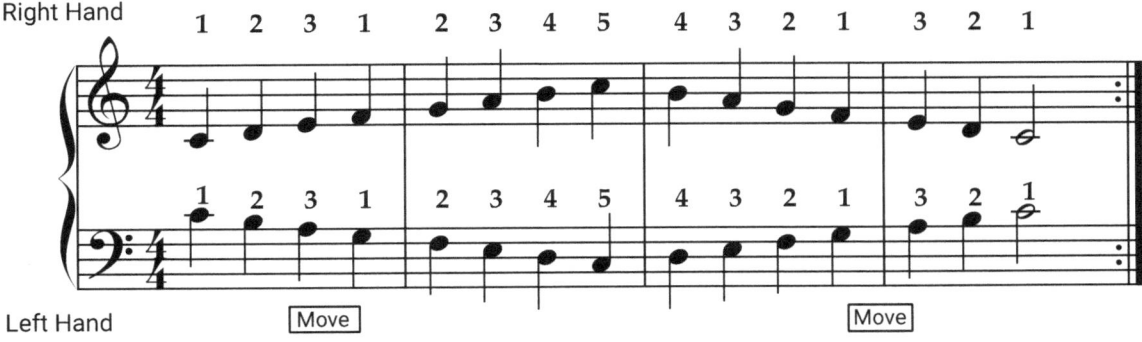

Dotted Notes and Melodies

Many melodies outline scales and the harmonies within scales. The major scale is the source of a surprising amount of music, especially melodies. Listen to this familiar Beethoven theme that we can use to demonstrate basic scale movement and learn about dotted notes at the same time.

A dotted note adds half the value of the note it follows. Play this example with the right hand in C position. The "Ode To Joy" theme is shown using half notes to help understand this concept easily.

Ode To Joy- half notes

In measure seven the dotted half note gets 3 counts. A half note gets 2 counts and half of that is 1. So 2 counts + 1 count = 3 counts. The E is held for 3 counts and the D is played on count 4.

Now the same example written in quarter notes. The first measure shows the counts in quarter notes and the second measure shows the counts in eighth notes- counted as 1 and 2 and, etc. Although you play quarters try to count twice as fast in eighth notes while you play the theme. A quarter note gets 1 count and half of 1 is 1/2. So 1 count + a 1/2 count = 1 1/2 counts. The E is held for 1 1/2 counts and the D is played on the "and" of 2.

Ode To Joy- quarter notes

There are often several ways to write a rhythm and it still sounds exactly the same. Here is measure 4 written in 2 different ways but played and counted the same. The first example shows the E with a *tie* that tells you to hold the quarter note and the eighth note together on the same note. The second example shows the same phrase with a dotted quarter. They sound the same.

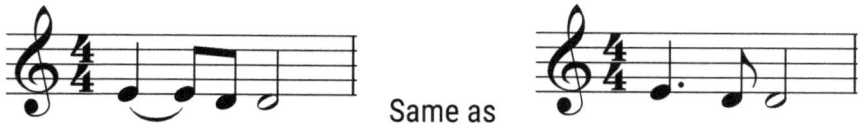

Same as

The major scales are really the most common scales used. They are where most of the common chords and harmonies we hear are found. Many other scales are also derived from the major scale.

Is there a popular song using dotted notes that follows a major scale note for note? There is. The Christmas carol "Joy to the World" by Handel follows a complete descending major scale, stopping on the strongest tones. They are the **chord** tones of the **tonic I chord** in C, the notes C, E, and G.

Joy to the World

A famous melody that follows the major scale is the "1812" Overture by Tchaikovsky.

1812 Overture

Another well known melody that follows a scale and uses dotted quarter notes is Greensleeves. The melody is minor and in the time signature of 3/4. Count only 3 quarter notes per measure and make sure to watch for the dotted quarters. For this example the complete fingering is shown.

Greensleeves

Scales are used to create music in an infinite variety of ways. One of many possibilities is to use **intervals** and skip notes instead of playing them in order. Intervals are explained on the next page.

Intervals- part 1
Major scale intervals

A musical *interval* is the distance between 2 notes and can be seen in various ways.
They can be played together or broken. When inverted they follow several rules.

Let's start with the *major scale intervals*. Here are the basic intervals of the major scale in C major:

Intervals can be played together:

unison   2nd   3rd   4th   5th   6th   7th   octave

Intervals can be played broken:

2nd   3rd   4th   5th   6th   7th   octave

There are some rules when inverting intervals. We'll explain these new intervals on the next page.

M2nd inverts to m7th   m3rd inverts to M6th.   tritone inverts to tritone   P5th inverts to P4th
Major inverts to minor   minor inverts to Major   tritone remains tritone   perfect remains perfect

Any interval added to it's inversion will total **9**. A *tritone* is a '4th and a half'. The tritone is so named because it is a distance of 3 whole tones{steps}. It also exactly divides the octave in half.

Intervals- part 2

Chromatic scale intervals

Now let's look at all the intervals within the octave using all 12 notes. The intervals are best understood by their relationship to the *Tonic* or *Root* of the key. The tonic of C major is the note C.

There are traditional names for these *Scale Degrees* but they are rarely used. Now the standard way to understand scale degrees is using *Roman Numerals*. We'll start with a simple illustration.

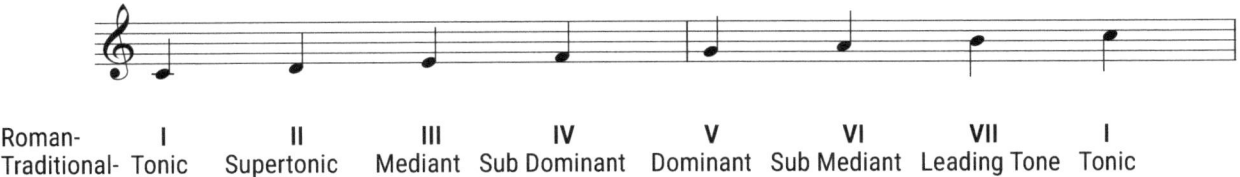

Roman-	I	II	III	IV	V	VI	VII	I
Traditional-	Tonic	Supertonic	Mediant	Sub Dominant	Dominant	Sub Mediant	Leading Tone	Tonic

The chromatic scale gives us every interval within the octave and their different qualities. There are some intervals that have several different names. Think of all of them as the distance from the root (or tonic) to another note. The larger the distance, the larger the interval. Here are the qualities.

Intervals made **smaller** by a half step are called *minor* or *diminished* and use a flat sign- 'b'.

Intervals made **larger** by a half step are called *augmented* and use a sharp sign-'#'.

The intervals of 4th's and 5th's are called *perfect* because of their strong *consonance* and their position in the *overtone series*. We'll have a thorough look at this interesting concept later.

From here onward we will use small case Roman Numerals and letters for minor qualities.

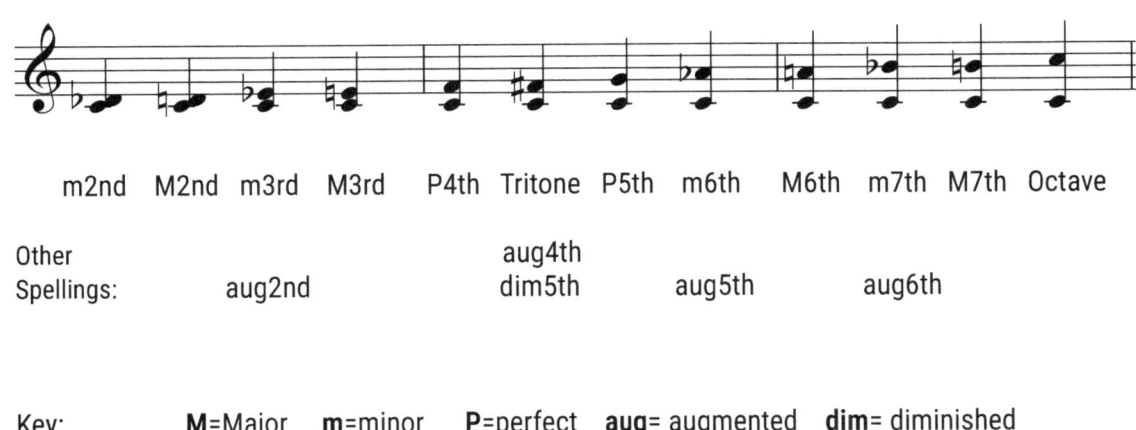

	m2nd	M2nd	m3rd	M3rd	P4th	Tritone	P5th	m6th	M6th	m7th	M7th	Octave
Other Spellings:			aug2nd			aug4th dim5th		aug5th		aug6th		

Key: **M**=Major   **m**=minor   **P**=perfect   **aug**= augmented   **dim**= diminished

The 12 Major Scales

The Sharp Keys

There are 12 major scales. They all follow the same patterns that we've seen in the C major scale. One such pattern is the tetrachord. Just knowing this one thing will help us build all 12 scales. Also the sharp scales all use the same fingering with just a few of them having small alterations.

If this is new or a little overwhelming there are ways to understand all of these scales as a group. We'll see those later in this chapter. For now just play through the scales to get acquainted.

The sharp keys in order are G, D, A, E, B, and F#. How to learn them all? We'll start by building tetrachords on the note and then play the scale in the right hand and left hand separately using fingering. First the tetrachords show the scale using **accidentals**, and then that scale is shown with it's **key signature**. The **double bar line** shows the end of each section.

The first scale with any sharps is G major. G has one sharp, F#, on the seventh of the scale. Start with the 4th finger of your left hand on G. Build a tetrachord- whole, whole, half step for the notes GABC. Skip a whole step and put your right thumb on D and build the second chord, DEF#G. Then play the scale separately in each hand. Remember an **octave** of the scale is 7 tones plus 1 played again. Think 7 + 1 = 8. Group these 7 notes using 3 fingers and 4 fingers. The **4th finger** plays **only once per octave**. Think 7= 3 + 4 or 4 + 3. The 5th finger ends or begins the pattern.

Play all the scales using this same approach, first as 2 tetrachords, then with the fingering shown.

G has one sharp- on F#

D has two sharps- on F#, C#

A has three sharps- on F#, C#, G#

E has four sharps- on F#, C#, G#, D#

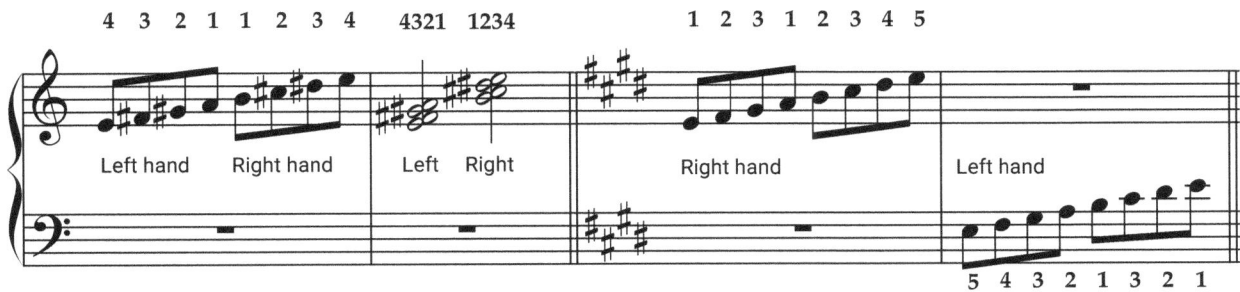

B has five sharps- F#, C#, G#, D#, A#   Observe the change of fingering in the left hand

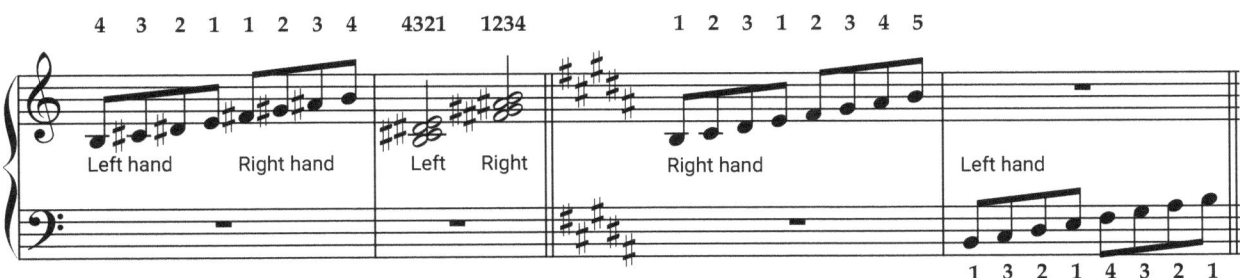

F# has six sharps- F#, C#, G#, D#, A#, E#(F)   Observe the change of fingering in both hands

The 12 Major Scales
The Flat Keys

By studying the sharp scales as a group it's obvious that there are patterns that connect them. If it seems a little confusing, it will be clearer as you move on at a relaxed pace. It's good to let all of these patterns develop naturally. Music has many patterns, and they can't all be seen right away.

There's a trick shown here for learning **all** the right hand fingering of the flat keys as a group.

F has one flat- on Bb   (C w/b7)

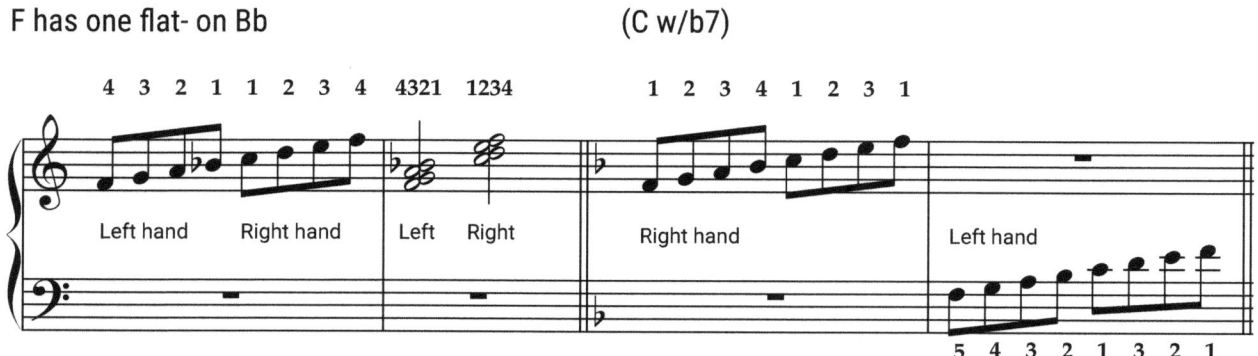

Bb has two flats- on Bb, Eb   (C w/b3, b7)

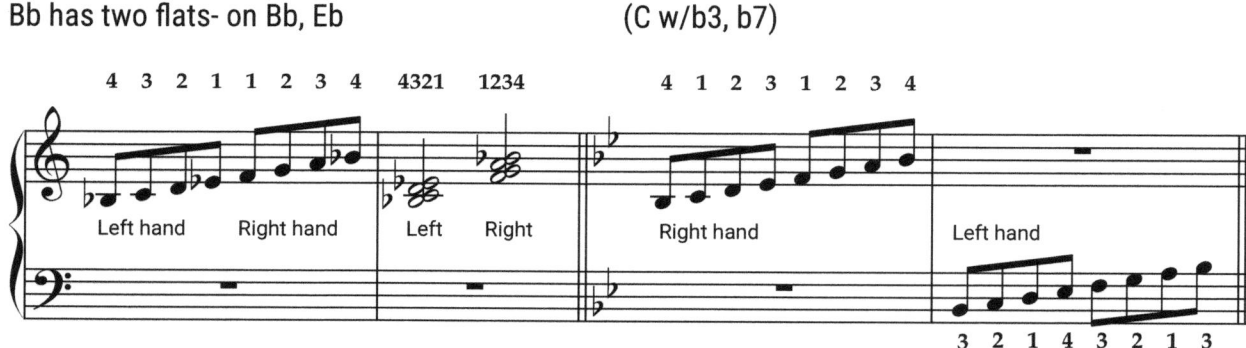

Eb has three flats- on Bb, Eb, Ab   (C w/b3, b6, b7)

Ab has four flats- on Bb, Eb, Ab, Db   (C w/ b2, b3, b6, b7)

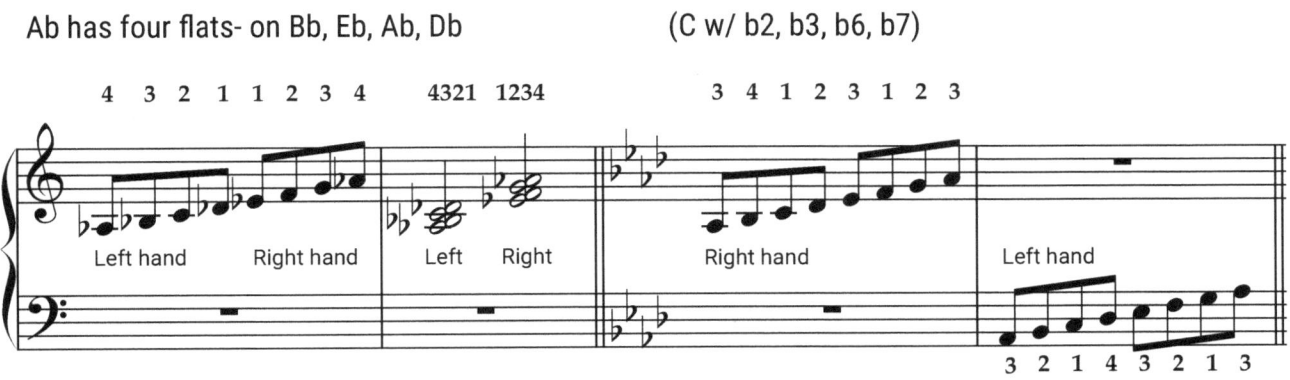

Db has five flats- on Bb, Eb, Ab, Db, Gb   (C w/b2, b3, b5, b6, b7)

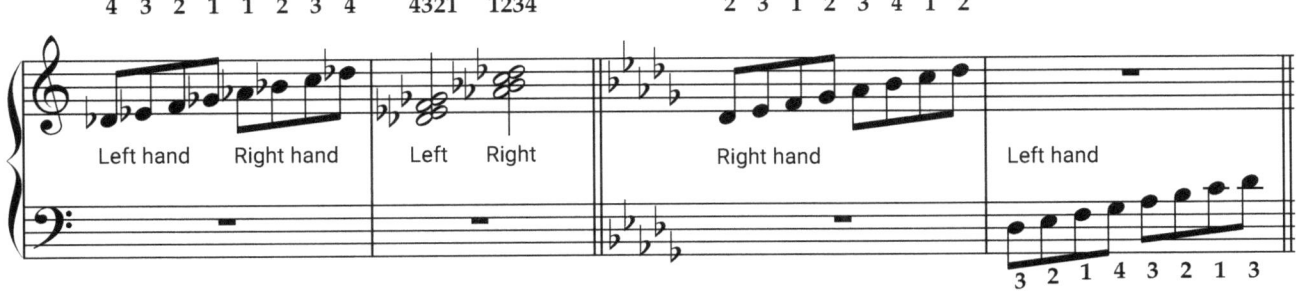

Gb has six flats- on Bb, Eb, Ab, Db, Gb, Cb(B)   (C(b) w/b2, b3, b5, b6, b7)

All of the right hand fingering for the flat scales has the thumb playing two white keys- C and F. Except for Gb, the key of six flats, which has a Cb (played as B) but still uses the thumb on a white key. Try to see **all** of the flat key fingering in the **right** hand as alterations of the **same C scale fingering** playing a group of 3 notes, then 4 notes, with the thumb always on C (or Cb) and F.

By playing all of these flat scales starting from C we're actually playing something known as a *Mode* of that particular scale. *Modes* will be covered in chapter four.

Key Signatures and Scale Patterns

The organization of the **key signatures** might seem overwhelming. How can one remember all 12? All those sharps and flats. Fortunately there is an easier way using **Intervals**. The first Interval we will use is the **5th**. We can just count up 5 in the **musical alphabet** and move up a 5th through all the keys in order. Remember the musical alphabet repeats seven letters, ABCDEFG.
Using the musical alphabet and the 5th interval we can line up all the **keys in order.**

Patterns for sharp keys

Start with C. Count **up 5** in the musical alphabet. C, D, E, F, G. The first sharp (#) key is G. Now count up 5- G, A, B, C, D. The next sharp key is D. Then count D, E, F, G, A. The next sharp key is A. Here's the pattern counting up the musical alphabet through to 6 sharp keys in order ending at F#.

Pattern for **sharp key signatures** in order. Count up a **5th** through the keys.

	CDEFG	GABCD	DEFGA	ABCDE	EFGAB	BCDEF#
Sharp Key	G	D	A	E	B	F#
Number of sharps In key signature	1	2	3	4	5	6

Here's another pattern for the **key signatures**. The first key with a sharp is G with one sharp. The sharp is F#, the 7th of the G scale. Think of this as a half step below the root of the key. F# is the **leading tone**- the 7th of G. Now move up to D keeping the F# and adding the 7th of D, which is C#.

Pattern for **adding sharps in order** to **key signatures**. Sharp the 7th- **leading tone**- of the scale.

Sharp Key	G	D	A	E	B	F#
Number of sharps	1	2	3	4	5	6
Change 7th to sharp	F#	C#	G#	D#	A#	E#(F)
Add previous sharps for sharps in order		F#,C#	F#,C#,G#	F#,C#,G# D#	F#,C#,G# D#,A#	F#,C#,G# D#,A#,E#

Patterns for flat keys

Moving to the flat keys and flat key signatures there are similar patterns.

Start again with C. Remember counting the musical alphabet backwards? Here's where we count **down 5** in the musical alphabet. C, B, A, G, F. The first flat (b) key is F. Now count down 5 from F. F, E, D, C, B. The interval of a 5th from F is **Bb**. So here we switch to flats. The next key a 5th down from Bb is **Eb**. Here's the pattern down the alphabet through 6 flat keys in order ending at Gb.

Pattern for *flat key signatures* in order. Count down a **5th** through the keys.

	CBAGF	FEDCBb	BbAGFEb	EbDCBAb	AbGFEDb	DbCBAGb
Flat Key	F	Bb	Eb	Ab	Db	Gb
Number of flats In key signature	1	2	3	4	5	6

Here's the other pattern. The first key with a flat is F with one flat. The flat is the **4th** of the F scale, Bb. In sharp keys we sharped the 7th but in flats we flat the 4th. It's an interesting coincidence that the 4th and the 7th scale degrees in the major scale are a tritone apart- exactly half an octave. Move down a 5th to the two flat key, Bb, and flat the 4th, Eb. Then down a 5th to Eb with three flats.

Pattern for *adding flats in order* to *key signatures*. Flat the 4th of the scale.

Flat Key	F	Bb	Eb	Ab	Db	Gb
Number of flats	1	2	3	4	5	6
Change 4th to flat	Bb	Eb	Ab	Db	Gb	Cb(B)
Add previous flats for flats in order		Bb,Eb	Bb,Eb,Ab	Bb,Eb,Ab Db	Bb,Eb,Ab Db,Gb	Bb,Eb,Ab Db.Gb,Cb

Although these patterns are all very helpful it's so much to remember. Especially with all 12 keys. Wouldn't it be nice if there was an easy way to see all of these patterns in one place? There is. On the next page.

The Circle of 5ths

The Circle of 5ths shows us all 12 keys and their relationship to each other using the 5th interval. The inversion of a 5th is a 4th. For this reason the circle of 5ths is also called the circle of 4ths. We'll soon use it both ways. The circle gives us some very powerful tools to connect the 12 keys. For example many common *root progressions* are available when using the circle, as we'll see.

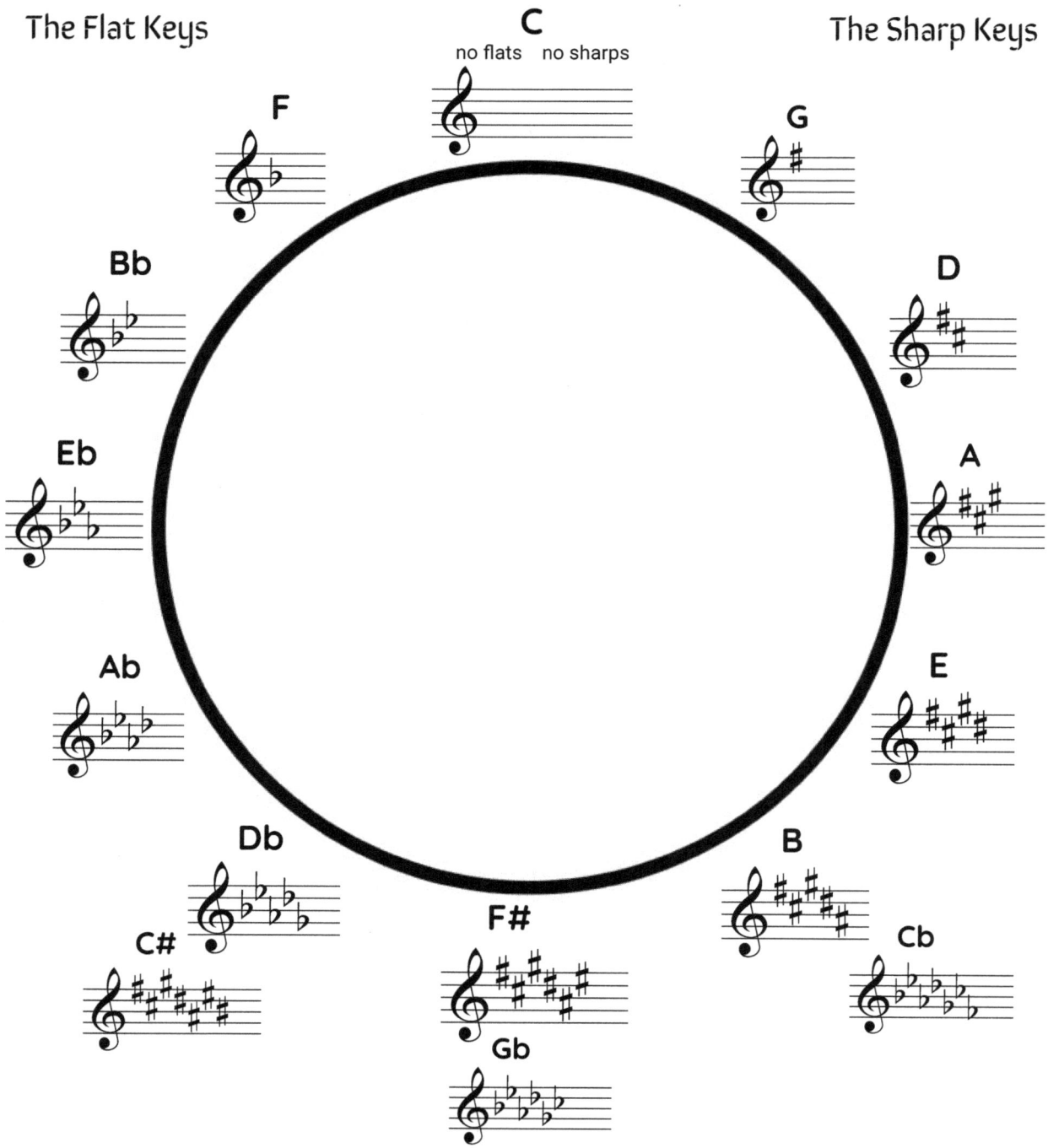

The Flat Keys

The Sharp Keys

Chromatic 5ths

Moving the 5th interval through 12 keys

On the circle of 5ths, imagine the 12 keys as numbers on a clock face with C at 12 o'clock. From C move **clockwise** for sharp keys or **counter clockwise** for flat keys, in order. Because of *enharmonic* spelling some say there are 15 keys, but there are really only 12. The *5th interval* is obviously important to learn. Now we'll use the chromatic scale to get to know the 5th in another way.

First play the chromatic scale with just the *thumb* of your right hand. Finger number 1. Start at middle C and play the chromatic scale for an octave up and down. *Sharps and flats stay in effect for an entire measure*. See how the natural sign restores a natural A in measure 2.
Right thumb only

Now play a *5th interval* with your right hand in middle C position. Your right thumb should be on middle C and your little finger on G a 5th above. Use fingers 1 and 5 for **all** the 5ths. Both notes will be the **same color**. Either the combination **white/white** or **black/black** in both fingers for all the 5ths **except** for the last two. The last 2 *positions,* **Bb** and **B**, are different. Bb is **black/white** and B is it's opposite, **white/black**. These are important differences so be sure to play them accurately. Play one octave **up and down** in the right hand. Use only fingers 1 and 5.

same color both fingers   w=white   b=black   2 different

After you can play it easily in one hand, play these 5ths with **both hands together** in parallel motion **up and down** for an octave or so. Use the 1 and 5 fingers in both hands, both ways, for all the 5ths.

The Minor Scales

The 3 Types of Minor Scales

There are 3 basic types of minor scales that can all be seen as variations of the major scale. Knowing the structure of the C major scale will be of great use as we learn all 12 keys. So learn the minor scales the same way and first look at them in C and then apply that knowledge to the other keys. It turns out that 1 of these 3 minor scales is within the major scale and so we have already played it. It's called *natural* or *relative* minor and played in C as a C major scale with a flat 3rd, 6th, and 7th scale degree. C *natural* minor is also the *relative* minor- the VI- of Eb major, a minor 3rd up.

The **A** *natural* minor scale is played like C major but starting on A- the VI scale degree- and is the *relative* minor of C major, a minor 3rd up from A. It's also called the *Aeolian mode* of C major.

Harmonic minor in C has a flat 3rd and 6th, using the natural 7th harmonically as the *leading tone*.

Melodic minor ascends with a minor 3rd and descends as a natural minor scale- with b3, b6, b7.

We'll continue by first learning all 12 major scales and then all the minors will already be familiar to us. The chapter on the *modes* of the major scale will further clarify our understanding of all the minor scales and help to see them as variants of the major scale.

The Whole Tone Scale

The 2 whole tone scales are created entirely with whole steps, or whole tones. There are 6 notes in each of the scales. If we start at middle C and move up in whole tones we get the following scale. There is no standard fingering for the whole tone scales. We can see this first whole tone scale as 3 white keys and 3 black keys.

Starting on C

The second whole tone scale does not include C. It starts on B or C#(Db), a whole step, and continues in whole steps. This whole tone scale can be seen as 4 white keys and 2 black keys.

Starting on B

It's also helpful to see the whole tone scales as a series of intervals such as major 3rds or tritones.

Ascending major 3rds

Ascending tritones

The Diminished Scale

The diminished scale is an 8 note scale. There are 3 diminished scales. They are built using a repeating interval structure of a *minor 3rd,* spelled as half step/whole step or whole step/half step, We'll start the first diminished scale on C using the half step/whole step pattern.

Start on C- half/whole step

Start on C with the whole step/half step pattern for the next diminished scale.

Start on C- whole/half step

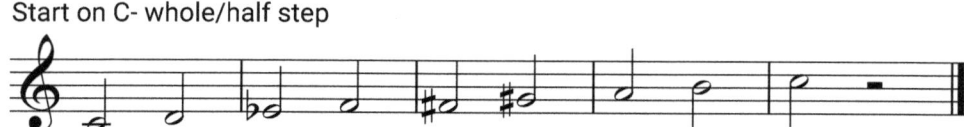

The last diminished scale doesn't include C. Start on B and use whole step/half step skipping C.

Start on B- whole/half step

Later we will closely examine the ways the diminished scale is used harmonically and relates to the diminished chord. There are many symmetrical patterns within this scale that we will look at. For now observe that the scale can also be understood as a series of *minor* 3rd or tritone intervals

The Chromatic Scale

Hands Together in Parallel and Contrary Motion

It is much easier to play the chromatic scale with the hands together than it might seem. Although more challenging pianistically it's a great way to use the visual and tactile aspects of the piano keyboard. The scale is again played here with just the **first 3 fingers** of each hand. The 2nd finger is **only** used where the **two white keys** are next to each other in half steps. Remember these two places on the keyboard are at E and F, and at B and C. It's actually fairly easy to see the hands moving together in *parallel motion* and the two places that use the second finger being played at **exactly** the same place and same time in both hands.

Play at least a couple of octaves or so **ascending and descending** with the hands playing **together**.

Remember the tritone? Start at each side of middle C with the left 2nd finger on B and your right 2nd finger on F- the tritone. Play the hands going away from each other and coming back in *contrary motion*. Play at least 2 octaves. The 2nd finger is used at the same time in both hands.

The tritone inverts as a tritone. So in the C scale it's between B and F **or** F and B. Although these two shapes look different on the keyboard they are both made up of the same 3 whole steps. Start with your left thumb on F and your right thumb on B- the tritone inversion. Play at least 2 octaves.

The Pentatonic Scale

The 2 basic scales- Major and minor

The pentatonic scale is a 5 note scale that is everywhere in music, and there are many types of pentatonic scales from all over the world. Here we'll start with the most common pentatonic scale known as the *Major pentatonic scale*. It uses 5 scale degrees, the 12356, from the major scale. In C major the notes are C,D,E,G, and A. By removing the 4th and 7th scale degrees we remove the tritone, the *dissonance* from the scale. In C the 4th and 7th are the notes F and B. By taking these notes out we are taking away any harshness in the major scale. It will always sound good. Play this up and down in the right hand over a C major chord in the left hand listening to the *consonance*.

Like the relative minor scale, we'll play a *minor pentatonic scale* down an interval of a minor 3rd from C. Start on A playing the same notes from C major pentatonic. Play them in the right hand up and down over an A minor chord in the left hand. Notice that although the quality of the sound is now minor it's still *consonant* because there is no tritone. If you prefer to think of scale degrees in A minor then think 13457, the same notes as 12356 in C major.

It might amuse you to know that the 'knuckle song' played on the black keys is pentatonic and outlines both the Gb major pentatonic and Eb minor pentatonic scales.

The Blues Scale

Major and minor

The blues scale is closely related to the pentatonic scale. And there are also two types- major and minor- just like with the pentatonic scale. Let's listen to the C major and c minor pentatonic scales over a major or minor triad. Scale degrees are shown above the notes for each example.

The c minor scale is the relative minor of the Eb major scale. The same is true for the pentatonic scales. The **c minor** pentatonic scale is the **same** scale as the **Eb major** pentatonic scale.

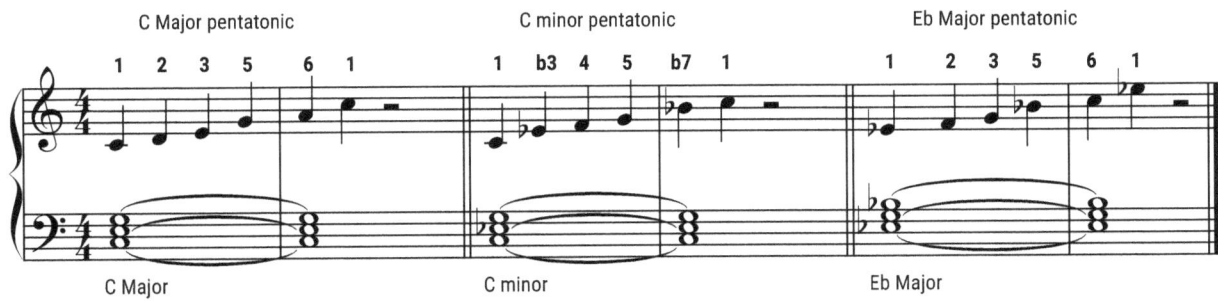

The blues scale adds a note to the pentatonic scale. Think of the major pentatonic scale degrees. Root, 2nd, 3rd, 5th, and 6th. There is an added chromatic *passing tone* between the 2nd and 3rd of the major pentatonic scale to create the major blues scale.

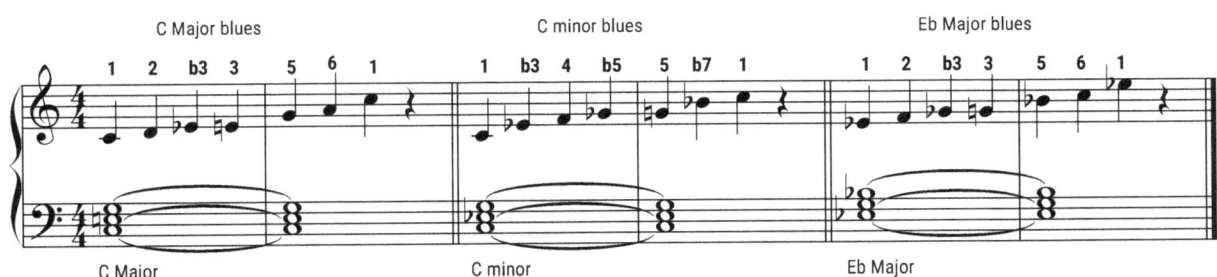

The c minor scale is the relative minor of the Eb major scale. The c minor pentatonic scale is the same scale as the Eb major pentatonic scale. They have this same relationship with the blues scales also. The **Eb major** blues scale is the **same** scale as the **c minor** blues scale.
Now play and listen to the C major and c minor blues scale over a voicing for a C7 chord.

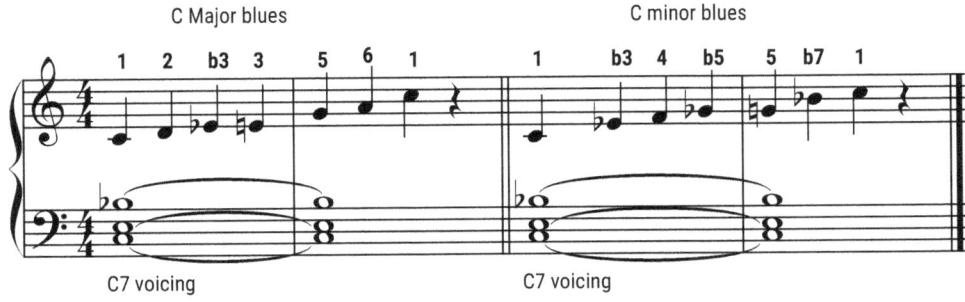

Let's finish this chapter with an approach to the blues using scales. As you have seen, the C major and the c minor blues scales both work when played over the same C7 chord voicing. Even though they have different qualities, when played over the 7 chord there is a kind of forgiving nature that allows quite a bit of dissonance. It is the nature of playing the blues that we work with creating dissonance and then resolving it. Now we will learn that combination in two other keys- F and G. Together the keys of C, F, and G will give us a I IV V progression in C. We can then play a C blues. More is explained about chords and Roman numerals in the next chapter. First just try these steps. Play these 6 different blues scales in the rh over a lh 7 chord voicing in the keys of C, F , and G.

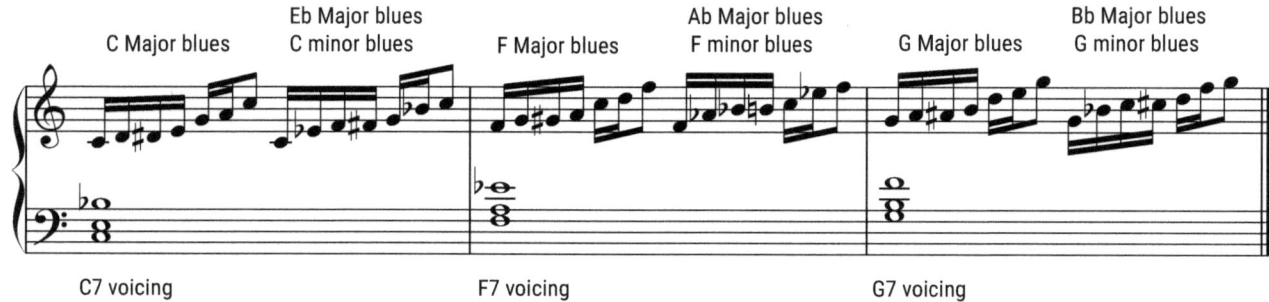

Then play this blues pattern- 5th, 6th, minor 7th, 6th- in the left hand for the keys of C, F, and G.

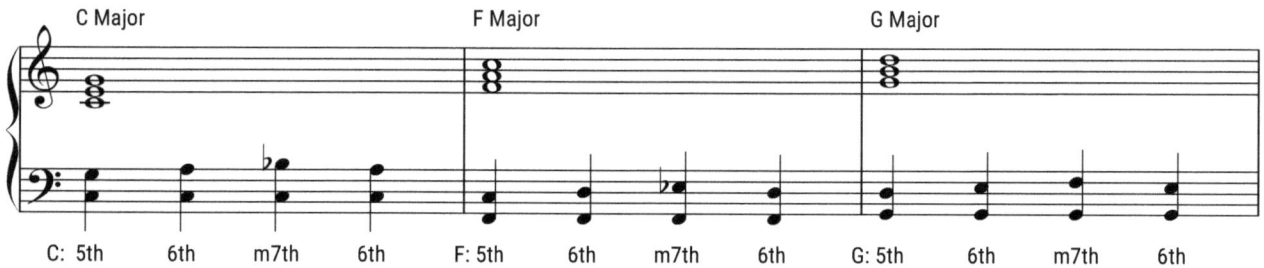

Ready to try playing the blues? Have fun playing around with these sounds in an 8 bar blues form.

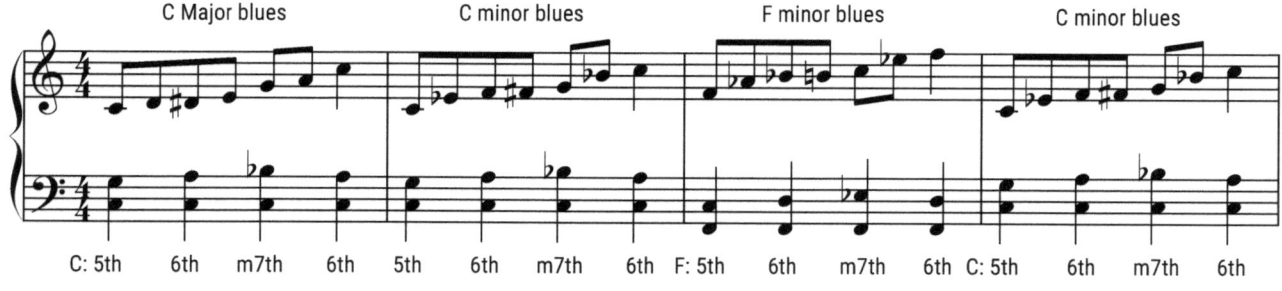

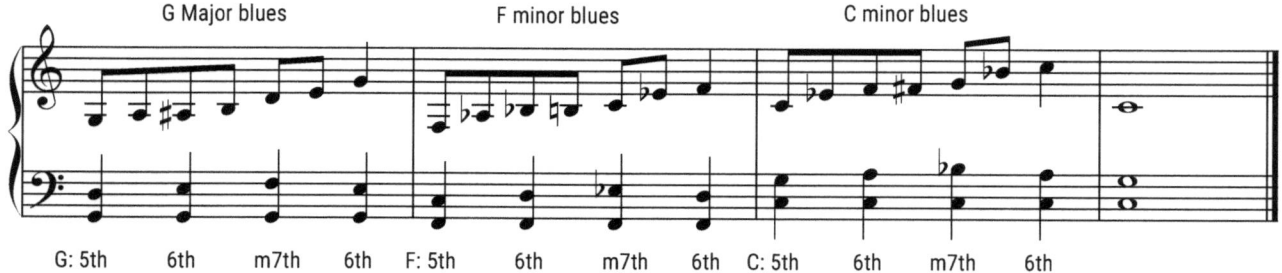

Pentatonic and Blues Scale Relationships

By now we have some idea of the 12 different keys and can play all 12 major scales. At this point we can learn several things at the same time making our time much more efficient. It's also a good opportunity to have a little fun while playing and absorbing the patterns of all 12 major **and** 12 minor scales together as a group. We'll do this by learning the pentatonic scales for every key. A huge amount of popular music uses these basic patterns. By learning them we are also developing the concept of the relative minor key and the relative minor pentatonic. The pentatonic scale has some more advanced potential that will be looked at closer in a later chapter. For now focus on combining it with the blues scale and quickly gain a practical knowledge of how to use scales musically in numerous playing situations. Work on understanding all 12 major and 12 minor scales at the same time. Take a little extra care here to study these two types of scales for each key, arranged as a group of all 12 using the clockwise circle of 5ths pattern.

With the right hand play the major pentatonic scale and then the relative minor pentatonic scale for each key as you move through the circle. Then play the two blues scales with the added *passing tone* and see them as the same scale in two different keys.

The harmonies are played in the left hand as regular major and minor chords, then using a 7 chord voicing for the blues scales. Listen closely to the scales and sound qualities in each of the different keys.

You will have a greater understanding of these patterns as you start to see them in all of the keys.

Think of the major pentatonic scale degree pattern as 12356 for each major scale.

Study this example carefully. C **major** has a relative minor, A minor, located a minor 3rd below C.
C **minor** is a minor 3rd lower than it's relative major Eb. The minor 3rd is obviously important.
In all examples the relative major pentatonic scale is shown above the minor blues scale.

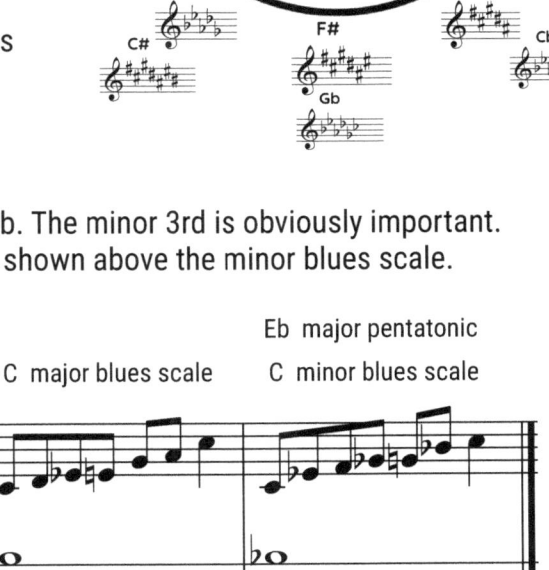

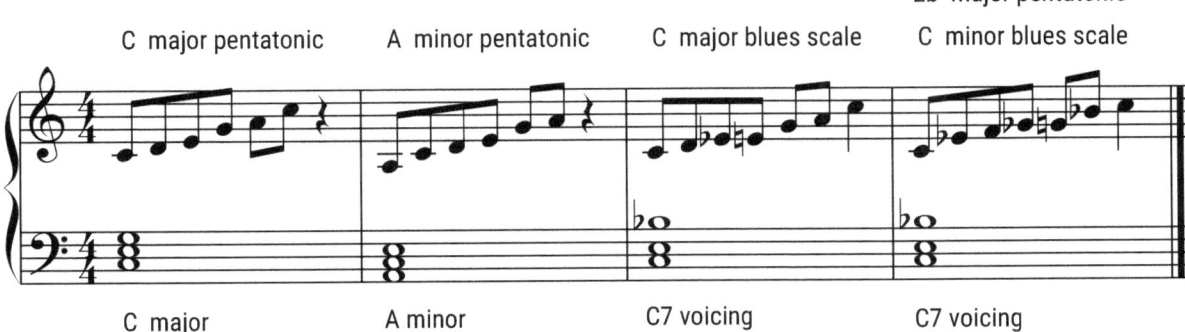

C major pentatonic   A minor pentatonic   C major blues scale   Eb major pentatonic / C minor blues scale

C major   A minor   C7 voicing   C7 voicing

You may have noticed in the previous example that on the circle of 5ths C is at 12 o'clock and the A and Eb are at 3 o'clock and 9 o'clock. A and Eb are equidistant from C, at an interval of a minor 3rd away in each direction.

Now see that F# is a tritone (or two minor 3rds) away from C at 6 o'clock. That would make sense, because a tritone is the interval that exactly divides the octave in half.

Here we can imagine a minor 3rd on the circle as a quarter 'slice' of a pie diagram, and then as a 90 degree arc of a circle. In geometry we might say these describe an x axis and y axis on a circle. With just a little imagination we can see these relationships are true for every key. Use the circle as needed moving clockwise through the 12 keys to help hear and learn them. Play carefully and not too fast.

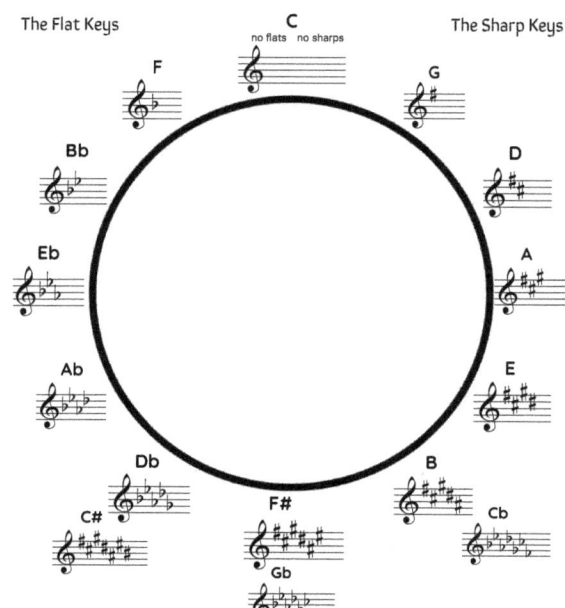

The Flat Keys   C   The Sharp Keys
                          no flats no sharps

G major pentatonic   E minor pentatonic   G major blues scale   Bb major pentatonic
                                                                      G minor blues scale

G

G major   E minor   G7 voicing   G7 voicing

D major pentatonic   B minor pentatonic   D major blues scale   F major pentatonic
                                                                      D minor blues scale

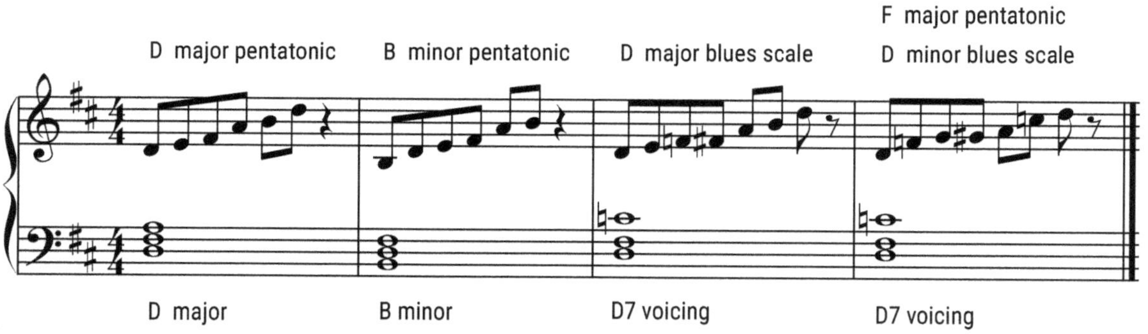

D

D major   B minor   D7 voicing   D7 voicing

A major pentatonic   F# minor pentatonic   A major blues scale   C major pentatonic
                                                                      A minor blues scale

A

A major   F# minor   A7 voicing   A7 voicing

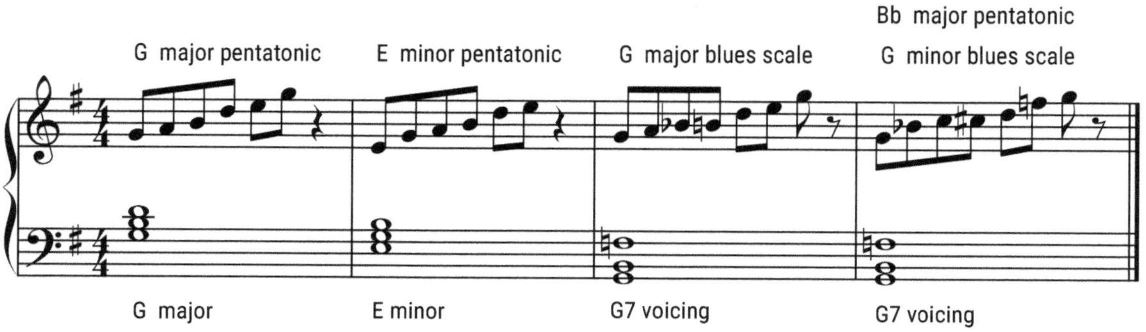

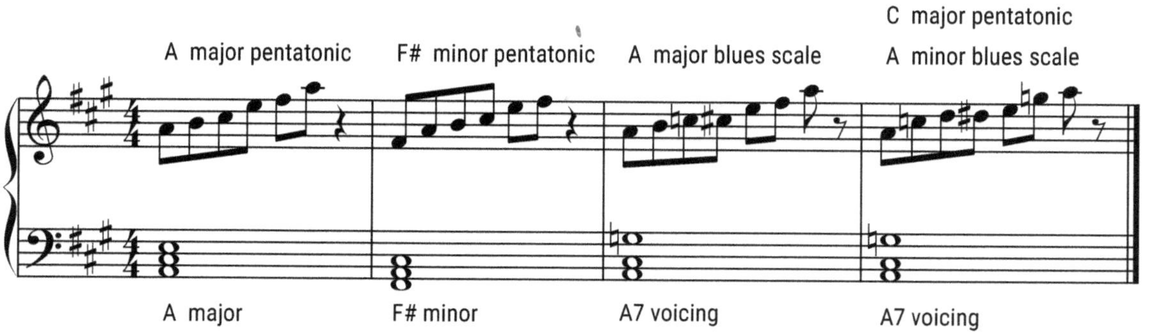

The Flat Keys
C
no flats no sharps
The Sharp Keys
F
G
Bb
D
Eb
A
Ab
E
Db
B
C#
F#
Cb
Gb

As we come up the other side of the circle and finish with F it's clear that some keys are easier to understand and play than others. So you should congratulate yourself now for making it through the most difficult thing so far. The process of identifying every key as unique has started and will become easier now because you are past the hardest part of the learning curve. You have familiarized yourself with **all** 12 keys and now it's a known universe. You have a full circle instead of any disorganization or confusion. We will be using the circle in both directions later on so let the pattern become a natural order in your thinking of the keys together. Learn them going clockwise and then try going counterclockwise.

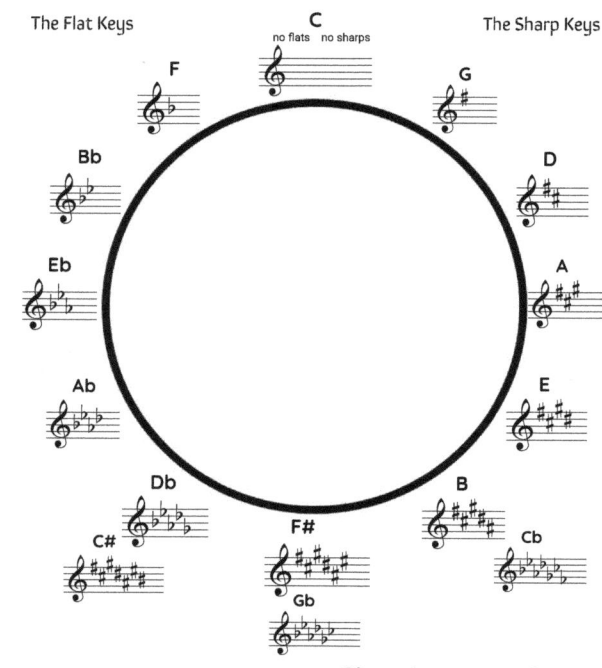

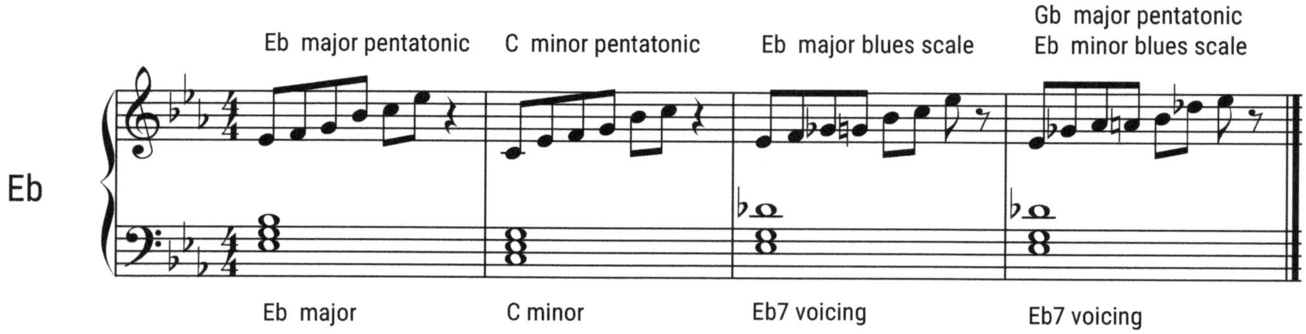

Eb major pentatonic
C minor pentatonic
Eb major blues scale
Gb major pentatonic
Eb minor blues scale
Eb
Eb major
C minor
Eb7 voicing
Eb7 voicing

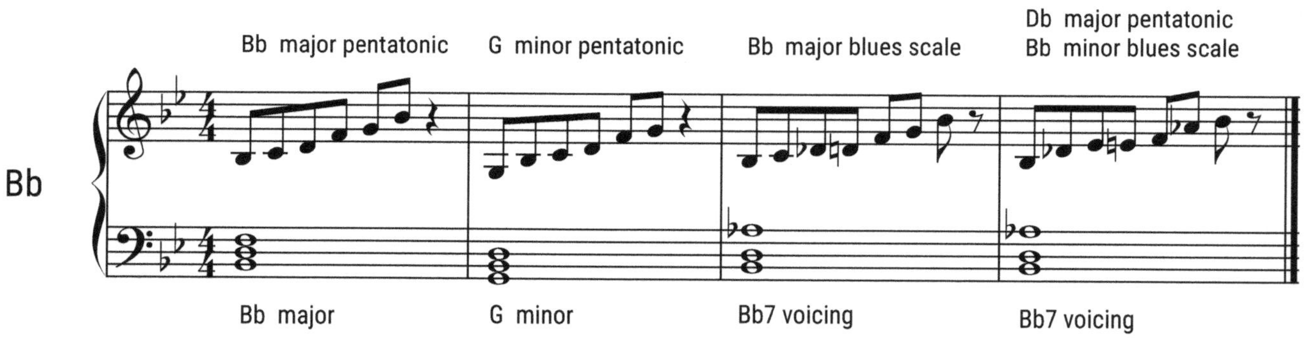

Bb major pentatonic
G minor pentatonic
Bb major blues scale
Db major pentatonic
Bb minor blues scale
Bb
Bb major
G minor
Bb7 voicing
Bb7 voicing

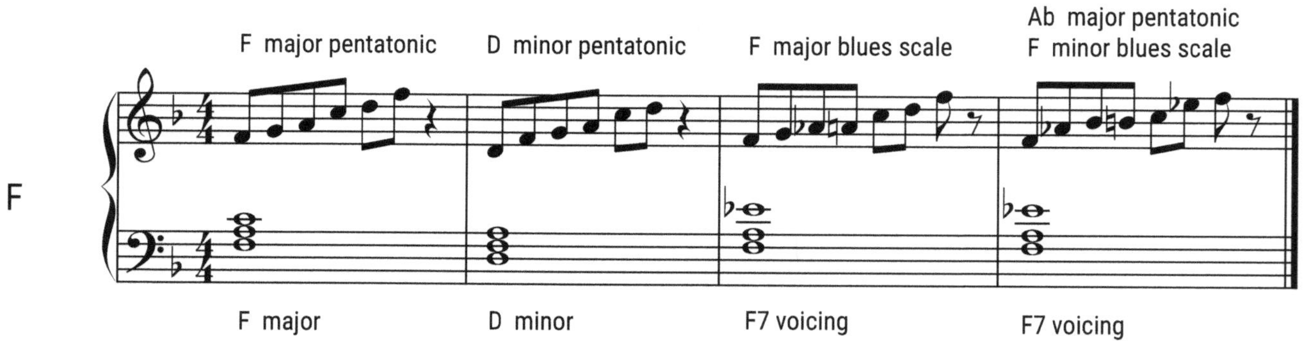

F major pentatonic
D minor pentatonic
F major blues scale
Ab major pentatonic
F minor blues scale
F
F major
D minor
F7 voicing
F7 voicing

Thinking About Chords- The 4 Basic Triads

The most common chords that are used in music are composed of 3 notes and are called **triads**. The building blocks of these common triads are the 3rd and 5th intervals. A good way to see a triad is that it is built with **two 3rds**. Another good way is seeing the outside interval of the **5th** and then a **3rd** in between these two outside notes. Know where the 3rd is located and also the quality.

There are two different types of 3rd intervals:
The **major** 3rd is composed of 2 whole steps.
The **minor** 3rd is composed of 1 1/2 steps.

The 4 basic types of triads

There are 4 basic types of triads. The **major, minor, augmented,** and **diminished** chords.

The **major chord** is composed of an outside interval of a 5th and a **major** 3rd in the middle. Also see it as two 3rds. First a **major** 3rd and then a **minor** 3rd. One of each type.

The **minor chord** is composed of an outside interval of a 5th and a **minor** 3rd in the middle. Again also see it as two 3rds. First a **minor** 3rd and then a **major** 3rd. One of each type.

Easy. Remember the **lower** 3rd in a major chord is **major**. The **lower** 3rd in a minor chord is **minor**.

The **augmented chord** is composed of an outside interval of an *augmented* 5th with a major 3rd in the middle. Also see it as two **major** 3rds.

The **diminished chord** is composed of an outside interval of a *diminished* 5th with a minor 3rd in the middle. Also see it as two **minor** 3rds.

The 4 basic triads in C

Major	minor	augmented	diminished
M3rd m3rd	m3rd M3rd	Maj3rd Maj3rd	min3rd min3rd

M=Major   m=minor

Using the 5th Interval to Create Chords

Building the most common chords- Major and minor

We see how the 5th interval is used frequently in the organization of music. It turns out the 5th is fundamental in building basic chords too. Here we'll use the idea of the chromatic 5ths from the previous chapter for something new and build **all** 12 major and 12 minor chords. A total of 24 chords that are the most common harmonies used in music. Play these chords first in their most basic shape, *root position*. The perfect 5th interval is used for every root position major and minor chord in all 12 keys. Since we have played that already we can simply add 3rds for the major or minor triads. When playing these chords it's very important to listen closely and identify the two different qualities for each *position*. We can build all 24 major and minor triads this same way.

The previous page showed how to build a major or minor chord in C by playing a major or minor 3rd in between the 5th. See how the minor 3rd is a half step smaller than a major 3rd, changing from a white key to a black key as it moves from E to Eb. This is the same process for all 12 keys. The minor 3rd is a half step smaller than the major 3rd without changing the outside interval, a 5th. Some teach the idea of 'happy' for major and 'sad' for minor to describe the qualities. That's unfair to minor but may help at first to subjectively identify the crucial difference between them.

The black key positions are shown in flats. The new *tie* symbol means **hold** the indicated notes (the 5th) for the duration of the combined note value (i.e. 2 quarters = 1 half).
Right hand only ascending and descending. Hold the 5th as shown and then add the **majo**r 3rd.

Then **change** all the chords to minor by **flatting** only the 3rd, holding the same 5th as in major. Note the Gb is an F# here. Make sure to read all of the other enharmonic spellings carefully.

Using the 5th interval to create chords- continued

Now play all chord shapes ascending and descending with **hands together** to learn all 24 chords.
Stay relaxed and let the right hand naturally teach the left hand using parallel motion.
We play these in a time signature of 3/4, so count 3 quarter notes per measure instead of 4.

Play an octave of major/minor chords **up** and then back **down**. Use 135(rh) or 531(lh) fingering.

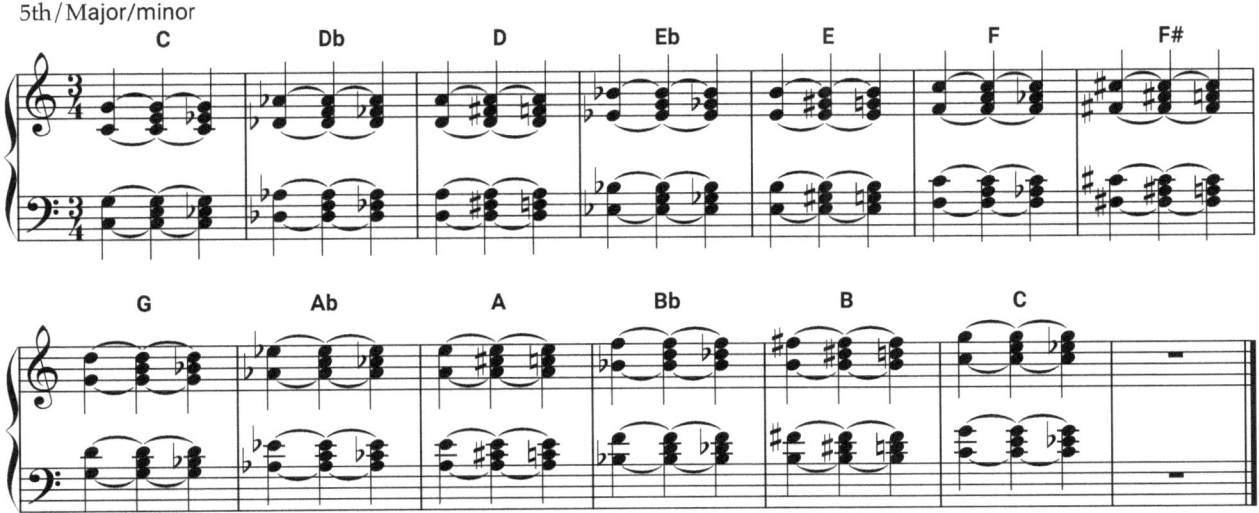

Then reverse the order and play minor/major. Same fingering in both hands for all positions.
Play an octave **ascending** and then **descending**.

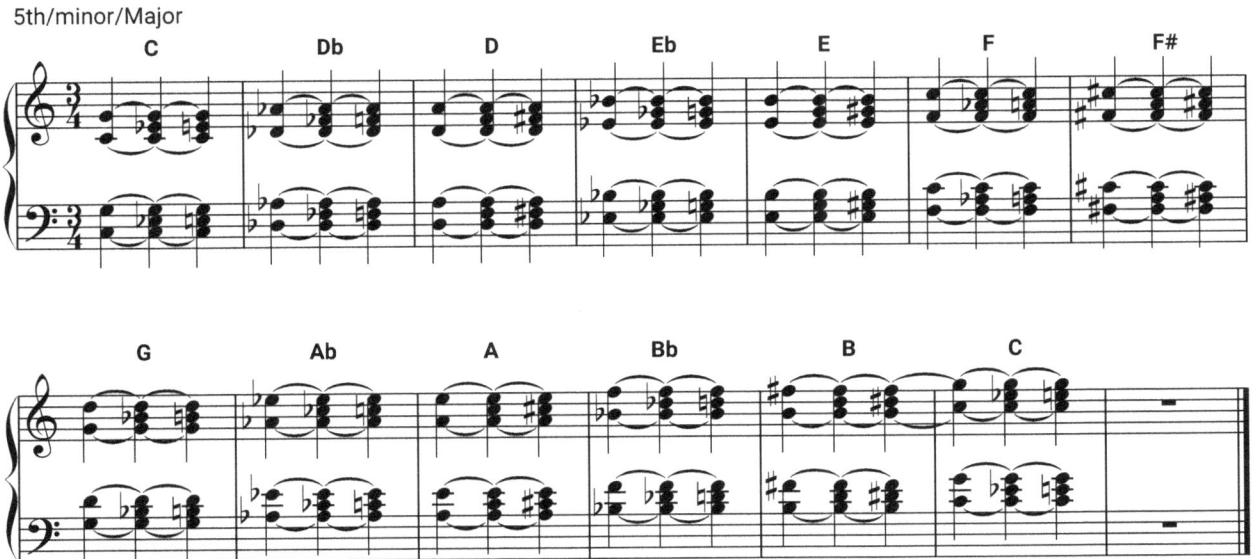

The 4 groups of Major triads

Using the piano keyboard to understand all 12 major chords

The **12 major triads** can be hard to understand at first because there are so many bits of information to process. 12 different chords might seem like a lot when first trying to understand them all at once. However, they aren't different in every way. We can see all of them as related if we first understand a few things to make it easier. They are all **major triads** and are built the same way structurally using intervals. A *major 3rd* and then a *minor 3rd* above it. One of each type. And since it's a **major** triad we can easily remember that the lower third is the major 3rd and the upper third is the minor 3rd. Also observe that the outside interval is *a perfect 5th* on all of these chords, as we saw earlier when we played them up and down chromatically.

Here is where the piano keyboard becomes an excellent way to understand all 12 shapes. We will use the color coordinated aspect of the keyboard and divide the 12 chords into only 4 groups. This is a much easier way to comprehend all 12 of them together and eliminate some potential confusion right away.

The 12 chords will divide into 4 groups of only 3 chords each.
Think of it like *4 x 3 =12*. Each group will be the same in color except for the fourth group.
Play through these shapes with the hands playing together to learn them by group.

The first group is **White, White, White** and contains the C, F, and G major triads.

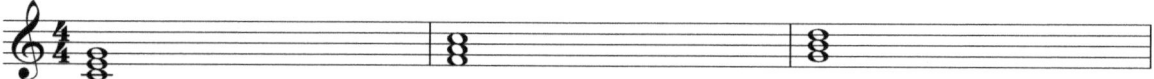

The second group is **White, Black, White** and contains the D, E, and A major triads.

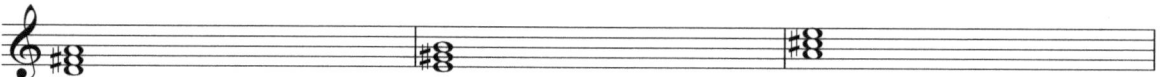

The third group is **Black. White, Black** and contains the Db, Eb, and Ab major triads.
An exact color reversal from the previous group.

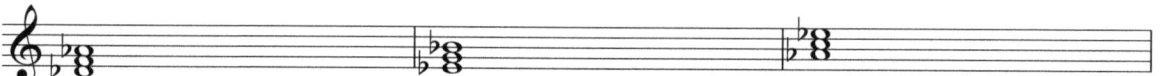

The fourth group is like a 'shoebox' since they are all unique one of a kind shapes and have their own special qualities.
F# (orGb) major is **Black, Black, Black**. It is a tritone away from C, exactly half the octave away, and it's exact color reversal.
Bb major is **Black, White, White**. B major is **White, Black, Black**, the exact color reversal of Bb.

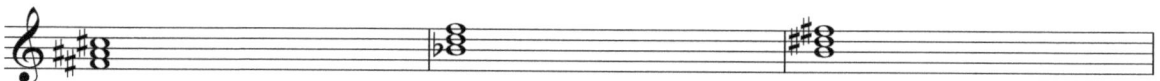

Using the 4 groups for minor triads

When it comes to playing 12 minor triads as a group there are some changes. Fortunately you have played them already using perfect 5ths so these shapes will be familiar to you. All use the 5th.

Change to minor by lowering the 3rd a half step. Now the qualities of the 3rds are reversed.
For a minor triad the lower interval is a **minor** 3rd and the upper 3rd interval is **major**.

Play these minor chords with the right and left hands separately and then together as a group.
W = white   B = black

The **first** group W/W/W becomes W/B/W and contains the C. F, and G minor triads.

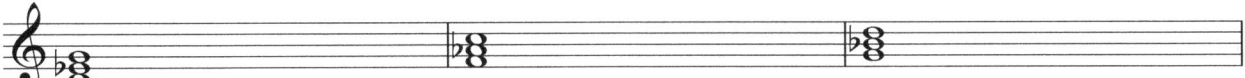

The **second** group W/B/W becomes W/W/W and contains the D, E, and A minor triads.

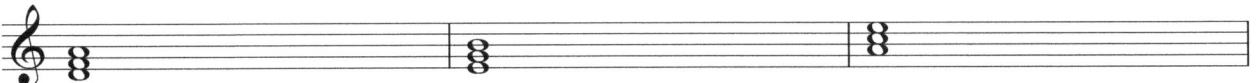

The **third** group is where the changes aren't so obvious except with Eb minor.
It contains the Db, Eb, and Ab minor triads. Listen carefully to each chord.
Watch for the enharmonic spellings. Fb is played as an E. Cb is played as a B.

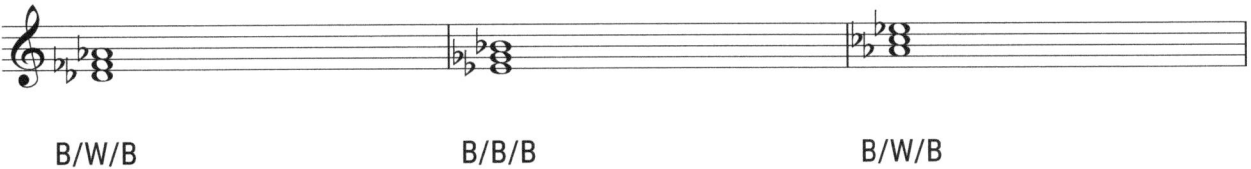

B/W/B   B/B/B   B/W/B

The **fourth** group has Bb and B minor still being color reversals of each other.
It contains the F#, Bb, and B minor triads. Again listen very carefully to these minor chords.

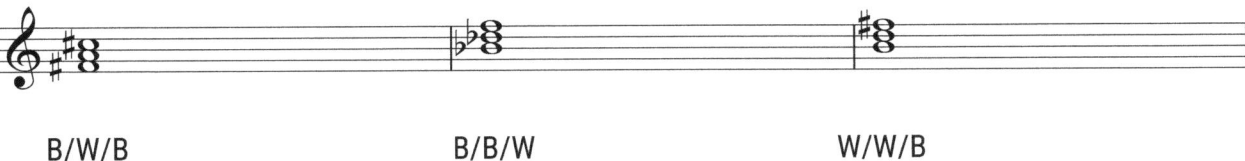

B/W/B   B/B/W   W/W/B

Chords and Scales

Let's put together the building blocks of **Harmony** and **Melody**. Typically melodies are in the upper register and played by the right hand on the keyboard. The left hand potentially has a great deal of power playing in the lower register by using harmony differently. For example, chord *voicings* that sound good in the high register might sound muddy when played lower. A great composer usually creates melodies for every instrument, even in a full orchestra, creating *simultaneous harmony* with the entire ensemble. Single notes can have tremendous musical power, especially in the bass. There are infinite ways to play melody over harmony, since they are two forms of the same thing. Think of a pool of notes, for example a major scale. We'll start with a basic combination divided by **the 4 groups** to make it easier. Play a major scale in the right hand *ascending* and then *descending* while holding the tonic I major triad in the left. Listen to the sequence of the sounds in the major scale and how strongly they relate to the tonic I chord. If something sounds unfamiliar but not necessarily wrong, you could be playing in a *neighboring* or *parallel* key. Make sure to play **all** of the accidentals shown in the key signatures for each key to hear the familiar major scale pattern.

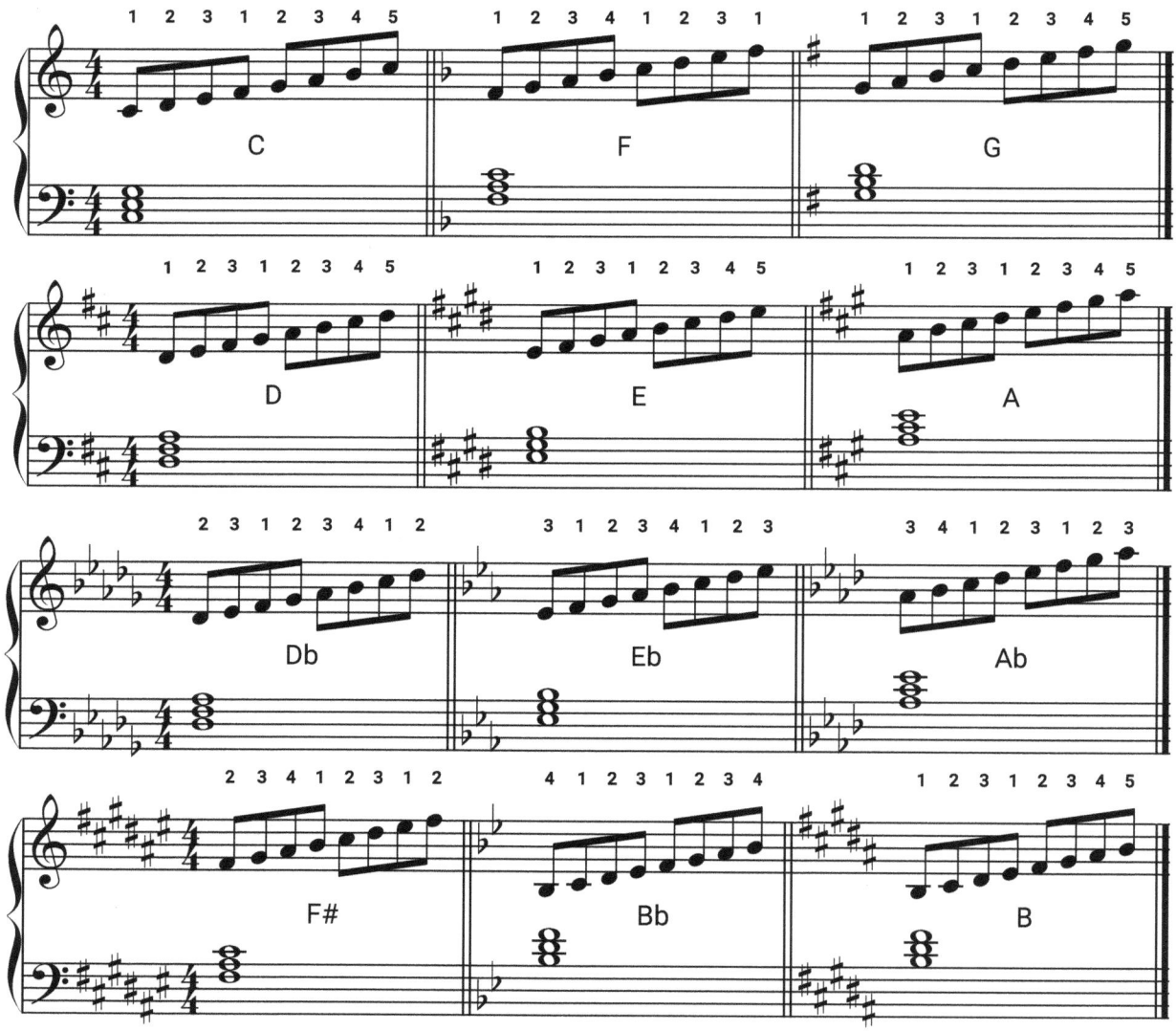

5 Finger Position in C

Hands Together

Put your right hand in middle C position, then put your left hand in C position an octave lower. Both hands now play the same 5 notes starting at C, followed by D, E, F, and G.

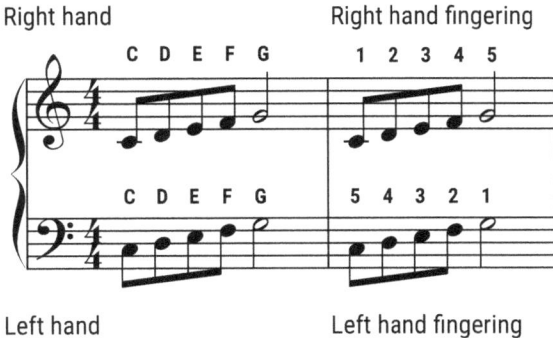

Begin playing the 5 notes using **contrary motion**. Start with the thumbs of both hands and then move the fingers one at a time playing each note towards the little fingers. Go back and forth from the thumbs to the little fingers playing the 5 notes in both hands. See how natural this movement feels. Our hands are acting like mirrors of each other. You can probably do this quickly, so go ahead and try to see how fast you can go.

Now try playing the same notes in **parallel motion**. The hands are playing the exact same notes at the same time starting at C and ascending to G, then descending back to C. Play these notes in parallel motion and see if you can go as fast as when playing them in contrary motion. You may experience quite a change in your ability to play the notes together in each hand accurately. It is almost like we are asking the left hand to rewire itself from what it is used to doing.

5 Finger Combinations

Hands together in C position

We can open up our musical thinking to new melodic pathways by creating some different or unusual combinations. We can build patterns that focus on **all** of the notes played by the 5 fingers.

Here is a one measure pattern followed by it's *melodic inversion* in the second measure.
This also shows us that the second group of four 16th notes is an *inversion* of the first group.

These 5 finger combinations are shown as four groups of four 16th notes per measure.
Fingering is shown for the first 2 groups which are played again to finish the measure.

Play the first measure only with both hands together in C position. Repeat it at least 10 times.

Then play the second measure and also repeat it at least 10 times.
Then play both measures with the hands together in C position using parallel motion.

Now let's switch to playing in minor by flatting the 3rd of each pattern. Change the E to E flat.
Remember accidentals stay in effect for the entire measure so continue playing E flat throughout.

It's possible to alter other notes like the 2nd's or 4th's so feel free to experiment with some of these more unusual sounds. Altering a pattern is a good way to make it more interesting or challenging to the ear.

These 5 finger patterns should all be played using the same process as on the previous page.
Again the second measure of each group is some type of melodic inversion of the first measure.
When finished with all of these as written, then play all of them in minor by flatting the 3rd to E flat.
After that feel free to experiment with altering the 2nd's and 4th's and listen to them.
No fingering is shown. That allows us a chance to develop our reading. Just read the notes.
The C position fingering remains the same for all of these patterns. RH 12345 LH 54321

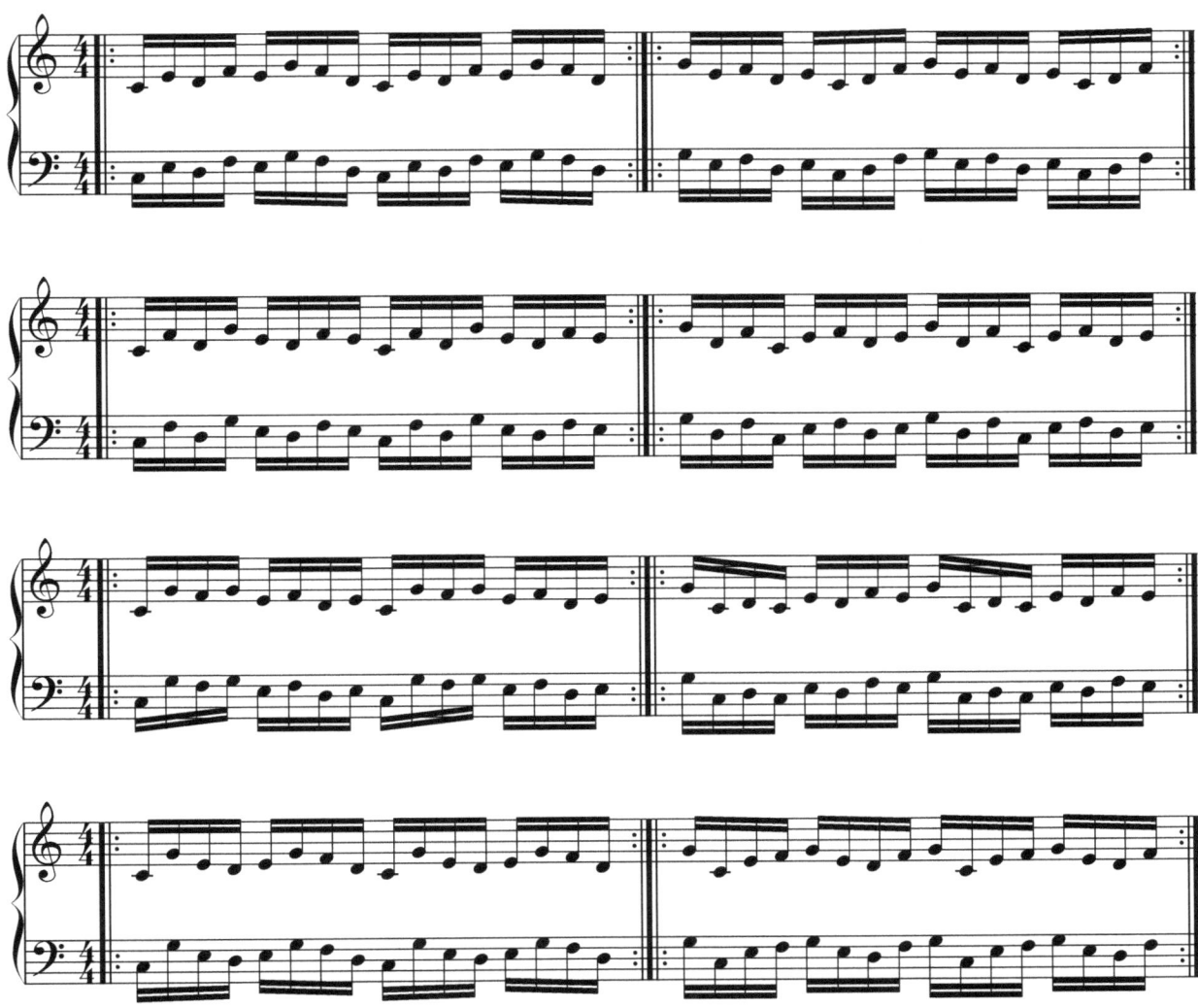

These examples are taken from Schmitt- Op.16, a series of technical studies for piano.

There have been many studies, or *etudes*, written based on patterns to be played at the keyboard.
Some are for specific technical purposes, for example focusing on a particular interval. Czerny
created many etudes that were written to assist in understanding and playing the music composed
by his teacher Beethoven. Hanon also wrote quite a few studies that are still used today to develop
certain specific techniques. Works by other composers like Clementi or Dohnanyi can also be very
helpful. Some etudes should be selected and introduced as a routine part of any deeper study.

All of the previous patterns should be played in every key. Here's how to do that using the 4 groups of triads as 5 finger positions for all 12 keys and applied to the first pattern we played.

After you have finished play all of these in minor by flatting the 3rd. Then take each one of the other measures from the previous page through all 12 keys using this same method with the 4 groups as 5 finger positions for each key. Make sure to also play all of them in minor by flatting the 3rd.

Triads of the Major Scale

There are seven different triads within the major scale. We will use large case Roman Numerals for major and small case for minor and diminished to show these scale degrees and their respective qualities. Remember, the diminished chord is composed of two **minor** 3rds.

The I, IV, and V chords are **major** triads.

The ii, iii, and vi chords are **minor** triads.

The vii chord is a **diminished** triad.

The fourth basic triad is not used. There is no augmented chord in the major scale.

Play through the C major scale using these chords in your right hand **ascending and descending**. Carefully listen to the qualities of each chord and the patterns they make together in the scale.

Right hand only 135 fingering.

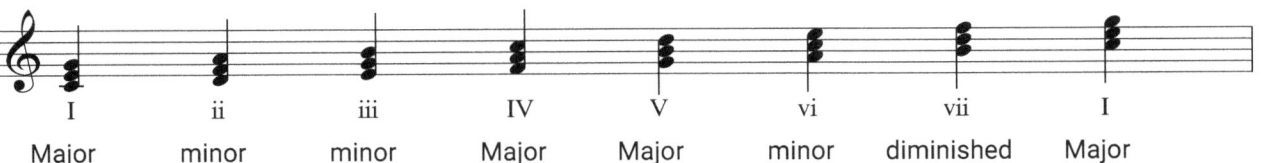

Then play ascending and descending using only the **Left** hand starting on the C an octave lower.

Now play them with the hands **together** an octave apart ascending and descending. You are now playing 6 sounds at once, 3 in each hand. Try to equalize each note so that you have a balance.

Hands together. 135 rh 531 lh. Stay relaxed and start slowly. Try to be accurate with every note.

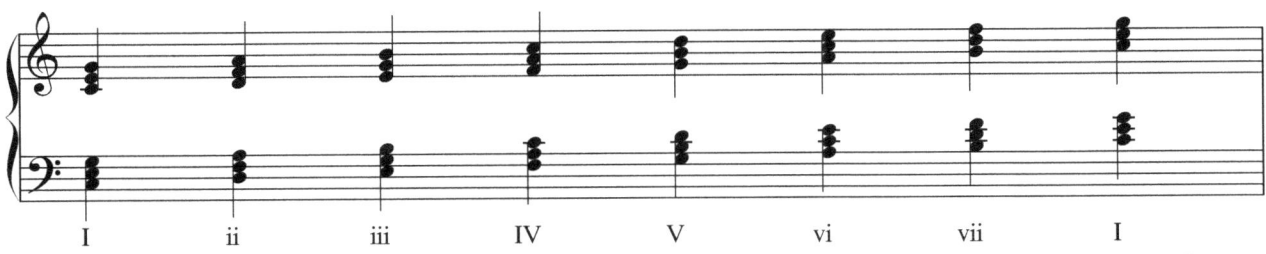

Keep the fingers the same distances apart playing through the scale. Speed comes from accuracy.

Transposing

Moving to Another Key

One of the best things about the piano keyboard is how it facilitates easy *transposition*. We can move a musical section or even an entire piece from one key to another for numerous reasons, the most important one being how it **sounds**. We often find that certain music only sounds good in certain keys. In practical terms the ability to move from one key to another is an extremely valuable skill when playing in an ensemble of any kind. For example a singer might have some difficulty with a particular key and want to take it up or down to a more comfortable one. The piano keyboard is set up perfectly to do this. On the piano there are visual, tactile, and aural differences between every key that individualize them and helps to identify their uniqueness. Many instruments do not have these same advantages. The 12 different scales can look and feel similar or even identical on them. The keyboard can help us to organize quickly and then *transpose*. Let's explore this idea.

We'll use the 4 groups to make it even easier to see all of these differences by the shapes and contours of each scale on the piano and that will help us to understand and organize all of them.

Begin with G from the first group. In the key of G, play the first four measures of this well known Minuet in G by J.S.Bach and we'll observe the melodic scale movement played in both hands.

Start with the right hand only on the 5th note in root position G (I) and play a melody based on the first 5 notes of the scale. Then the hand moves to the IV position of the scale, in this case C, and starts on the 3rd note and plays the rest of the scale using a *melodic sequence* based on the first melody. Watch for the F# in the key signature, the 7th scale degree, played at the end of measure 3 by the right hand. The entire musical phrase ends with an octave played on G, the tonic of the key. It also outlines the correct fingering for the key of G, with the thumb playing the root and the 4th.

Play the left hand only and listen to the part by itself. The left hand plays an *accompaniment* starting with the tonic I chord and continuing with a counter melody that also follows the scale. Now play the hands together and see that this piece was created by the composer to teach their students about the G major scale. The complete piece is a masterclass in outlining a key and taking a musical journey through some very interesting harmonies and related keys.

We'll return to play the complete version of this wonderful Minuet later. For now *transpose* just the first 4 bars through the 12 keys using only the I and IV positions within each key.

Moving on to the next 2 keys in this group, pay close attention to the changes in the sound. After transposing these first 4 measures of the Minuet in G to another key, what is your reaction? Does it make the piece sound any better or worse to you?

Transposing to the key of C you'll notice the similarities with G right away. The fingering is the same. All the moves are the same for both hands. The only change is there's no sharp on the 7th scale degree in the right hand as it now outlines the C major scale.

Play in C- hands separately and then together.

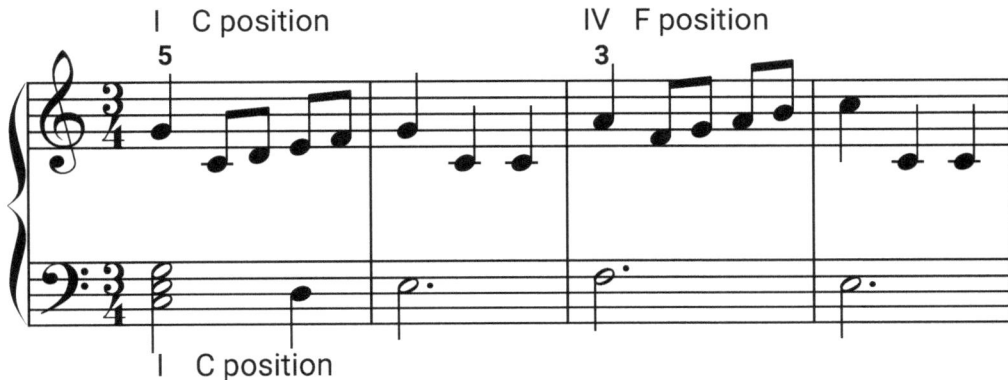

In playing F, the last key in this group, we can see some changes. There is a flat on the 4th scale degree, Bb. However for these examples we'll continue using the same fingering for all 12 keys. The F scale uses other fingering, as we have seen. But for now we are only looking at the structural changes between each key and using just 2 five finger positions- the I and IV, So keep it easier and make as few changes as possible to see and feel the distinct contours and shapes of every key.

Play in F- hands separately and then together.

Continuing on, the I and IV positions are shown in each example for every key. Remember both positions outline major triads on those scale degrees. The 5 notes played on the IV position in the right hand sound like a major scale but with a raised 4th scale degree. This is the *Lydian* mode of that particular scale. Modes are explained in the next chapter..

Play hands separately and then together. Watch for all accidentals in the key signatures of the various keys.

Group three
(Db),Eb,Ab

Group four
Bb,B,F#

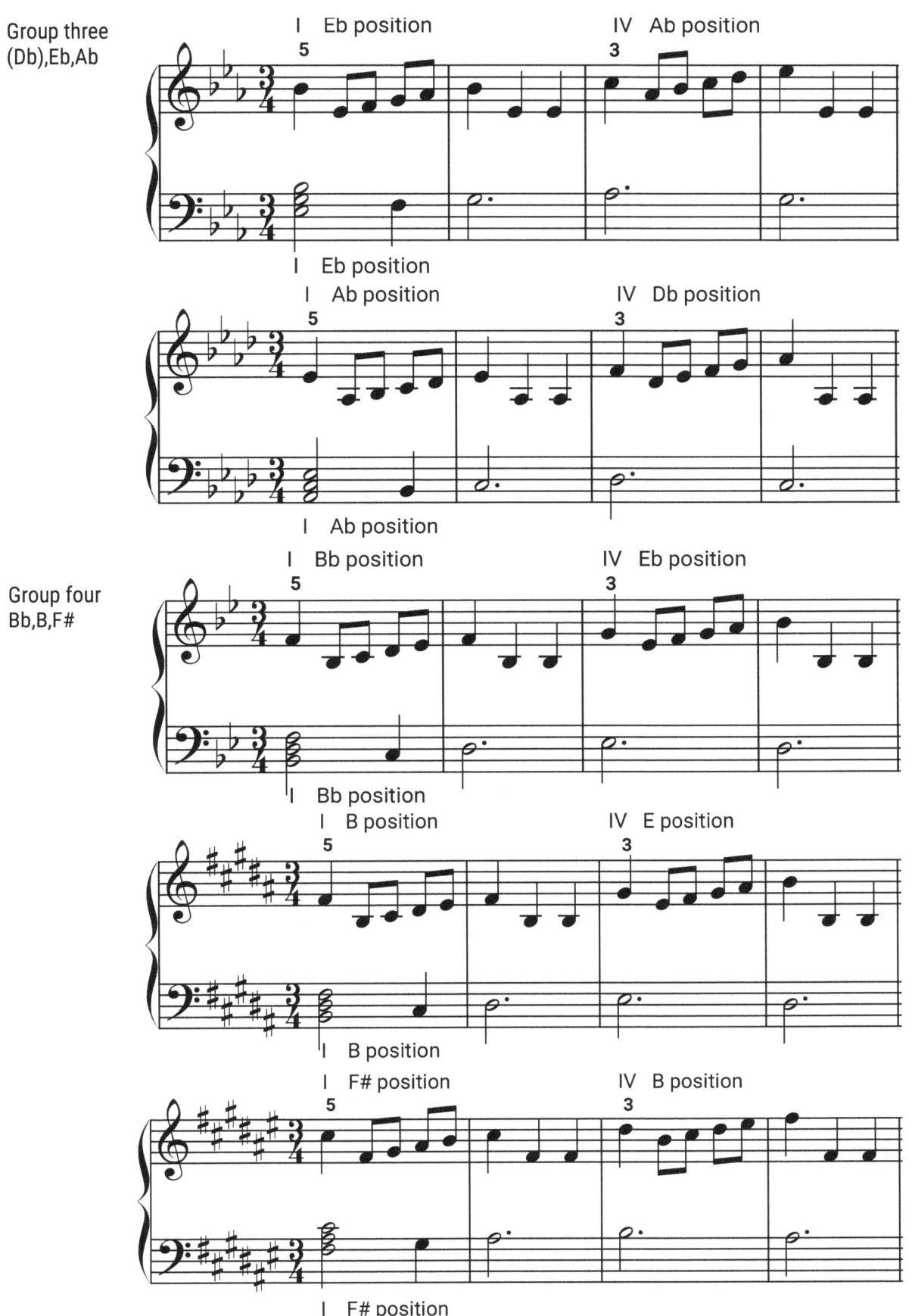

Building a Chord Vocabulary

Having learned the 7 basic chords in the major scale we can do a little calculating. There are 12 keys and 7 chords for each key. 12 x 7 = 84. We know most of that already. 6 of those 7 chords will be major or minor and we have already built all 12 major and 12 minor chords using the 5th interval. They're familiar to us. It's important now to know where each chord sits within a key. For example the I, IV, and V chords will be major in every key. To make this much easier we'll work on just 3 keys at a time using the 4 groups of triads as the I chord of each key. This is an excellent way to learn a scale that's immediately practical- how it really gets used in music. Watch for **accidentals** in the key signatures especially as you move through the harder keys and listen carefully to be sure that you play the familiar **chord pattern**- shown in C but it's the same for all the keys. Go slowly with the hands separately and then together ascending and descending.

Try the two tetrachords as needed for understanding the shapes and contours of any scale.

Use 135 rh and 531 lh for all chords and listen carefully to the I-vii pattern in all keys.

2nd group

D

E

A

3rd group

Db

Eb

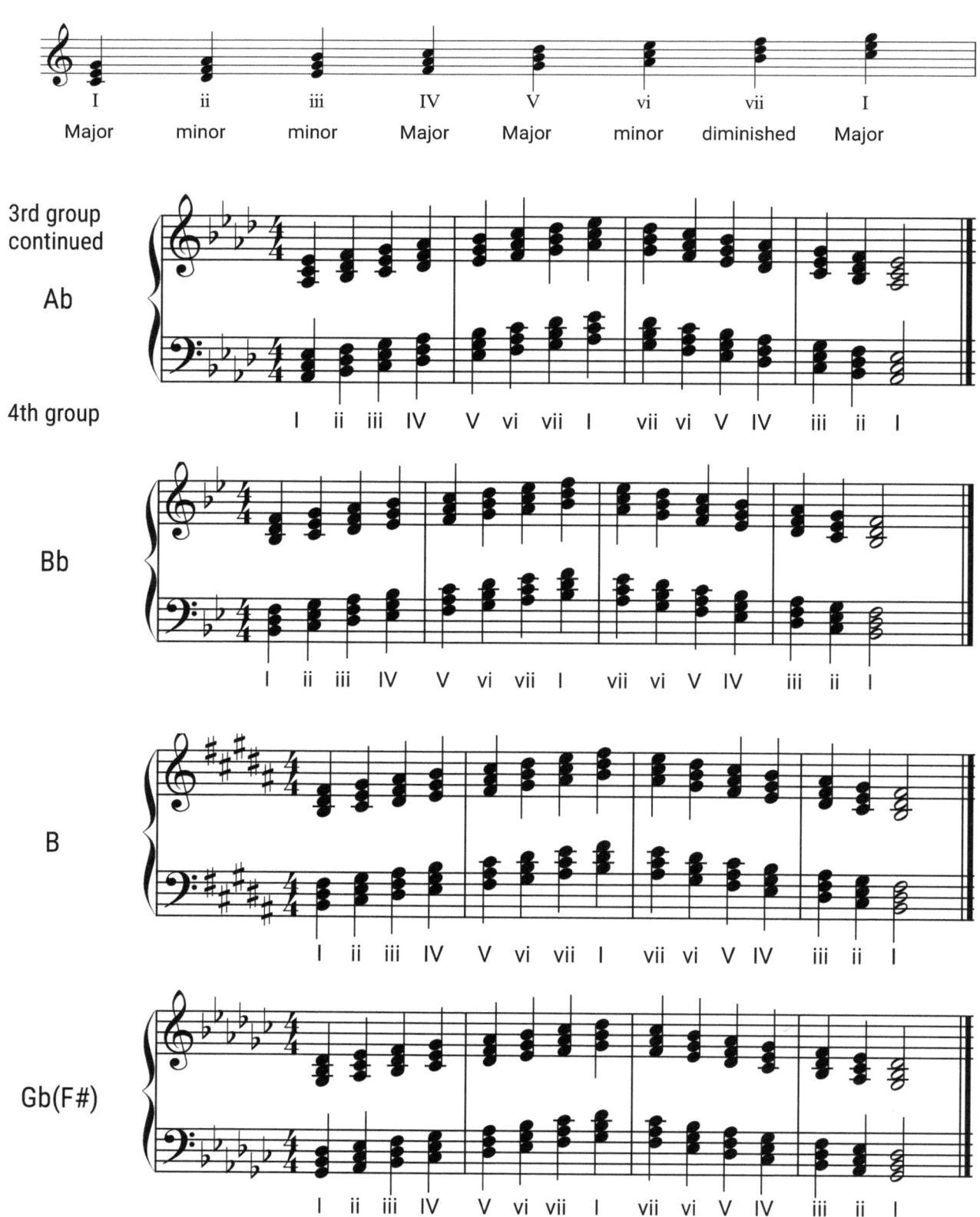

3rd group continued

Ab

I　ii　iii　IV　V　vi　vii　I　vii　vi　V　IV　iii　ii　I

4th group

Bb

I　ii　iii　IV　V　vi　vii　I　vii　vi　V　IV　iii　ii　I

B

I　ii　iii　IV　V　vi　vii　I　vii　vi　V　IV　iii　ii　I

Gb(F#)

I　ii　iii　IV　V　vi　vii　I　vii　vi　V　IV　iii　ii　I

Try the two tetrachords as needed for understanding the shapes and contours of any scale. Use 135 rh and 531 lh for all chords and listen carefully to the I-vii pattern in all keys.

Using the Whole Tone Scale

Patterns for moving through 12 keys

There are 2 whole tone scales. Each one is composed of six notes that move up or down by whole steps. We can apply this pattern using parallel motion and quickly move something through six keys at the same time. This sequence has been extensively used musically, so it will sound familiar to you. We can use this pattern to get all of the basic chord shapes under our fingers. Watch out for the enharmonic spellings. Remember that accidentals are in effect for an entire measure unless changed by another sign. Listen carefully and sound equally **all** the notes moving in whole steps. Play hands separately, then together, ascending **and descending**. Use 135 rh 531 lh for all chords.

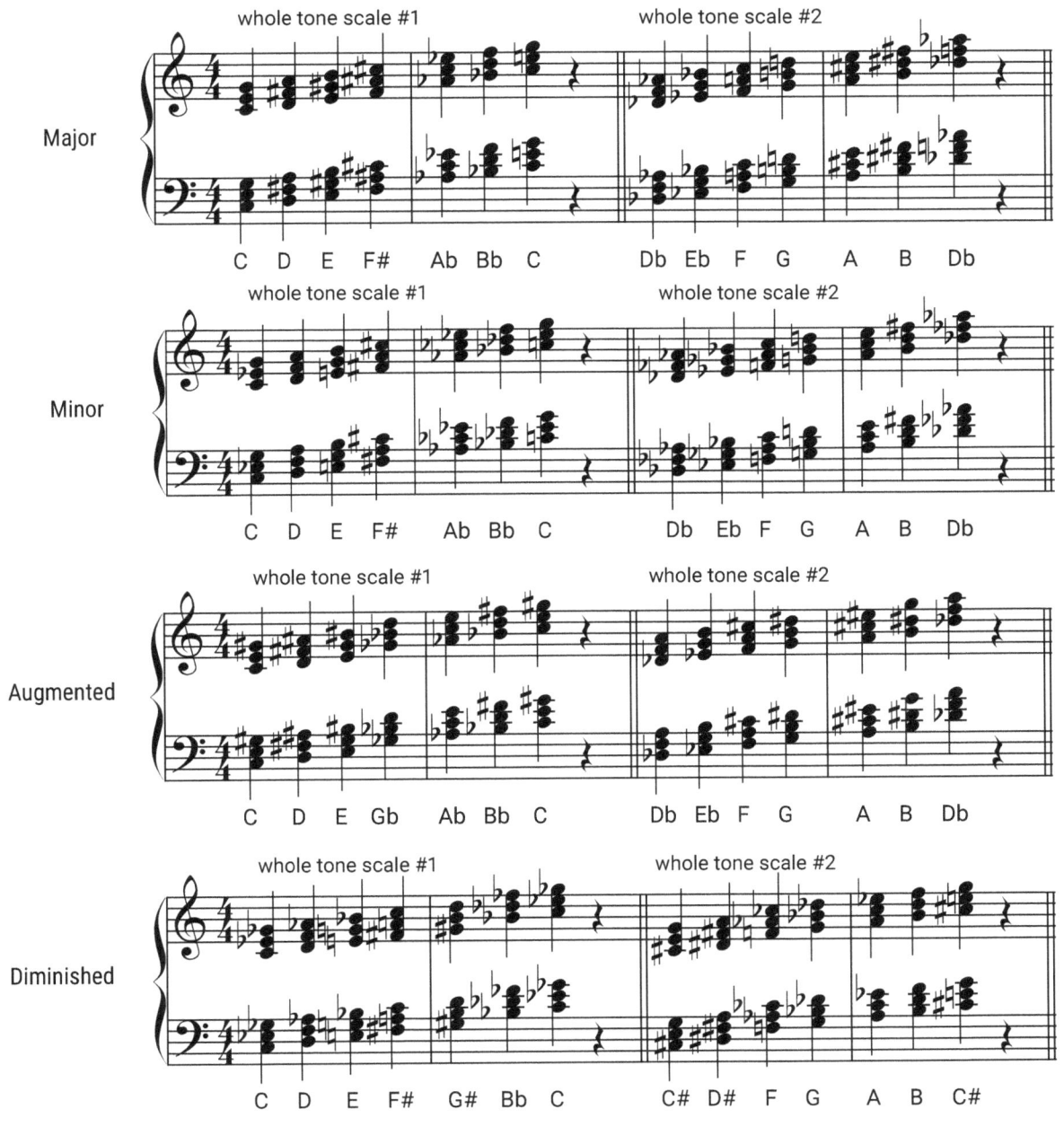

Left Hand Root Patterns– Circle of 5ths

Counter clockwise

Using the circle and reversing directions is an excellent way to play all 12 notes of the chromatic scale in the left hand. This requires minimal effort and allows us to move quickly. We can use the circle clockwise or counter clockwise with a reversing pattern and easily move through all 12 keys.

The **counter clockwise** pattern is also extremely useful as a practice pattern because it outlines the root patterns found in three very common *chord progressions*. The **V I, ii V I,** and **vi ii V I** are progressions we encounter everywhere in music. Playing something counter clockwise through the circle includes all of these patterns for all 12 keys. So common root progressions are something you can practice at the same time when going through the keys, making your time more efficient. The fastest way to improve is to take something through all 12 keys and if possible try to practice more than one thing at the same time. Consider this a good root pattern for the left hand.

The left hand moves up a 4th from C and then down a 5th repeating. Use 41 or 51 fingering.

up 4th/down 5th

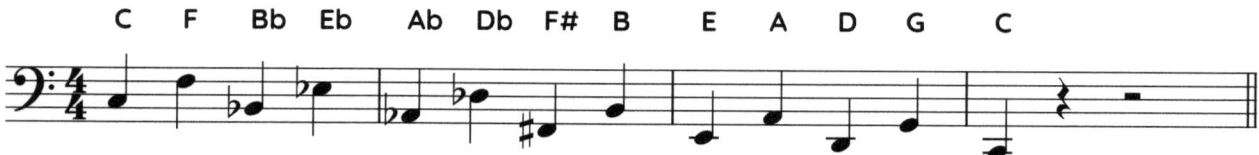

Now the other direction, approaching C from G and then down a 5th through the circle repeating.

up 4th/down 5th

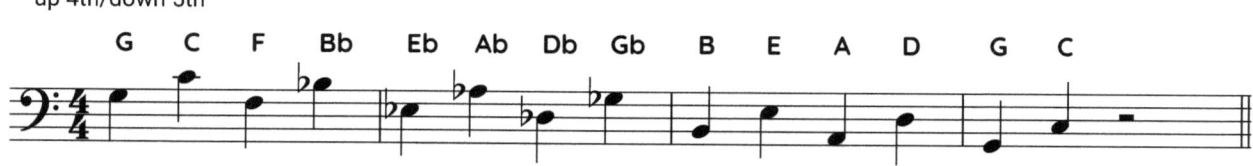

If these patterns have a familiar sound, they should. There's another pattern that follows every other note. Pick either the upper or lower *voice* and you'll see a familiar friend. These notes all follow the whole tone scale, which can also be seen as a series of tritones (3 whole tones).

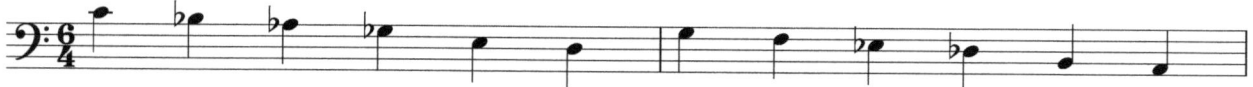

We'll use this counter clockwise pattern throughout this book because it does more than just one thing. Using it to take something through all 12 keys will always sound musical because it follows a familiar sequence and keeps the sounds fresh. The next example will demonstrate this.

Play the following example and listen to this potent augmented chord going through all 12 keys. First try it in half steps using the chromatic scale as a pattern and then try the counter clockwise pattern. Listen to how the 4th chord in the first sequence -Eb- already loses it's 'bite', and we still have 8 more keys to go. Our ears are bored already. But in the second example the Eb still has the 'bite' even though it's played in the exact same place as the 4th chord in the first sequence. And all of the following chords retain that potency through the rest of the keys. Our ears like this better, so when we use the circle to take something through the keys we'll use it counter clockwise.

Right hand. Some new ledger lines, accidentals and enharmonic spellings so read these carefully.

Left Hand Root Patterns- Circle of 5ths

Clockwise

This is another pattern to be played in the left hand moving clockwise through the circle. Although it doesn't outline the same common patterns as going counter clockwise this other pattern is used extensively in certain types of music, and it's another good way to go through all 12 keys. Make sure to start an octave lower to give the left hand room to ascend. The left hand is now moving up from C using a 5th interval. This pattern outlines basic triad shapes and common root-5th bass patterns. Once again the upper or lower notes will follow the whole tone scale. Use 51 fingering.

And the other way. Approach C from F. Same pattern, up a 5th down a 4th. Use 51 fingering.

Using the Circle of 5ths with Triads

After learning the root patterns for the left hand it's time to try playing the 4 basic triads through all 12 keys. Great progress is made by taking something through all of the keys. It allows us to see many things at once and process a huge amount of information. Although it may seem 12 times slower at first, later on it's much more than 12 times faster. We'll try using the counter clockwise pattern as a root pattern in the left hand with the 4 basic triads in root position in the right hand. Right hand use 135 for all chords. Left hand use either 41 or 51. Watch for enharmonic spellings.

Sus4 and Add2 Triads

Triads without 3rds

There are triads that have no 3rd interval to define a major or minor quality. Using the interval of a 5th and another type of interval we can build two new basic triads. This other interval can be seen as either a 2nd or a 4th interval away from the root. Both of these two new triads have an open quality because there is no longer a major or minor 3rd to outline either of those strong harmonies.

The first triad is called a **Suspension** or just **Sus** or **Sus4**. It is called that because it has a sound that suspends any basic perception of major or minor **tonality**. There is no 3rd to do that.
This chord can be thought of as a 5th interval combined with a 4th interval as the suspension.
Play in both hands as a root, 4th and 5th going counterclockwise in the circle of 5ths.

Play with the hands together 2 octaves apart using 145 rh 521 lh. Move up a 4th and down a 5th.

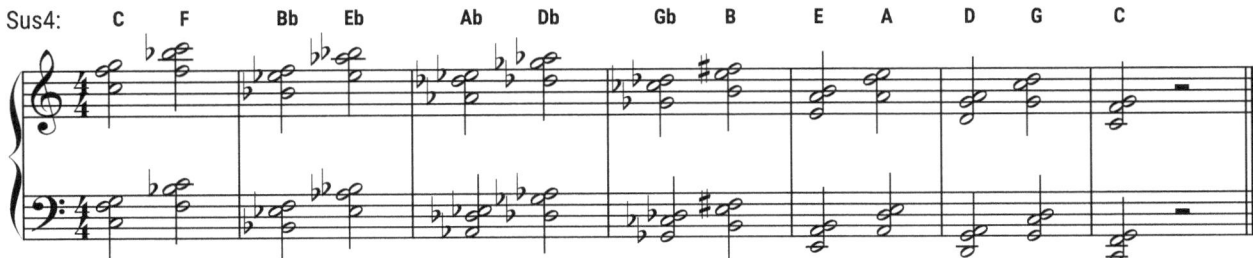

The second triad is called the Add2 chord. It also suspends any major or minor qualities but in a different way using the 2nd interval rather than the 4th like in the Sus chord.
This triad can be thought of as a 5th interval combined with a 2nd interval as the suspension.
Play in both hands as a root, 2nd and 5th going counterclockwise in the circle of 5ths.

Play with the hands together 2 octaves apart going through the circle using 125 rh 541 lh.

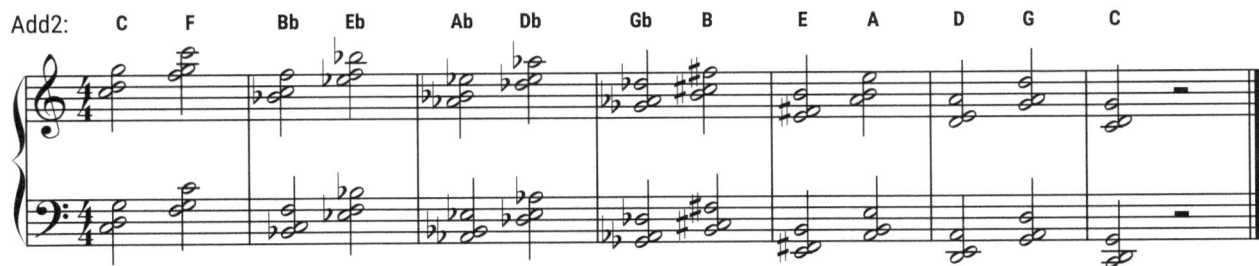

Both the Sus and the Add2 chords are used quite a lot in popular music. They increase and extend the harmonic vocabulary of other chords when used in combination with them. We will see later on how the sound of the suspension is really in it's own category and has many uses.
However, suspensions are often used to resolve to a more conventional sound.
Next we will look at some examples of resolving these suspensions to major or minor.

Sus to Triad Resolutions

Resolving Sus4 suspensions to Major and minor triads

The Sus chord has a unique quality that can be used musically in a variety of ways. There are some musical compositions that build on just Sus chords. However there are even more that usually resolve the suspension in some way back to a basic major or minor tonality. We can show how this is done in many musical situations with a basic illustration resolving a Sus triad to a major or minor triad. There are many ways to to play with these two sounds working together, and in the hands of a skilled composer they represent an entire family of harmony. Learning these two sounds of suspension and resolution and how they work together will increase your understanding of these principles while playing and listening to all kinds of music, regardless of style. We will come back to these two sounds in more detail later on. For now play through the basic shapes.
Play the Sus-Major combination in the right hand using 145 changing to 135 fingering.
Play the root pattern in the left hand using 41 or 51 fingering.

Play the Sus-minor combination in the right hand using 145 changing to 135 fingering.
Play the root pattern in the left hand using 41 or 51 fingering.

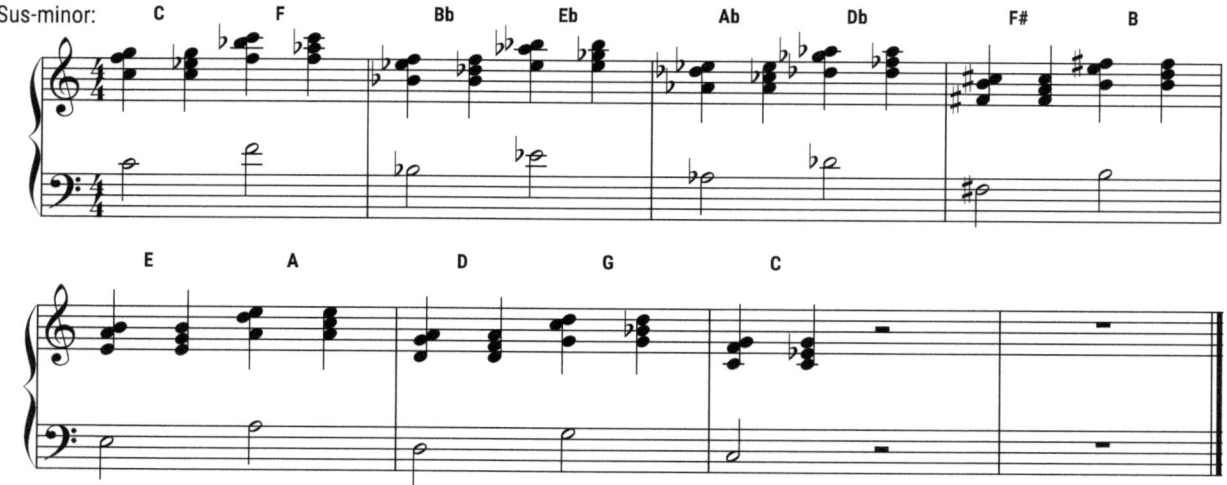

Add2 to Triad Resolutions

Resolving Add2 suspensions to Major and minor triads

Many popular songs use a suspension of the 2nd. In more advanced harmonies it is considered the 9th, which is the next larger major scale interval after the octave. More on that later.
For now just play through the basic combinations and learn the pattern of the circle.

Listen carefully to the difference between the Sus chord you just played and the Add2 chord.
Hear how they resolve to a major or minor triad. The Add2 can be used as a chord substitution for many different chords in a playing situation because it sounds strong but doesn't clash with either a major or minor sound. These two chords have a close relationship as we'll see on the next page.

Play the Add2-Major combination in the right hand using 125 changing to 135 fingering.
Play the root pattern in the left hand using 41 or 51 fingering

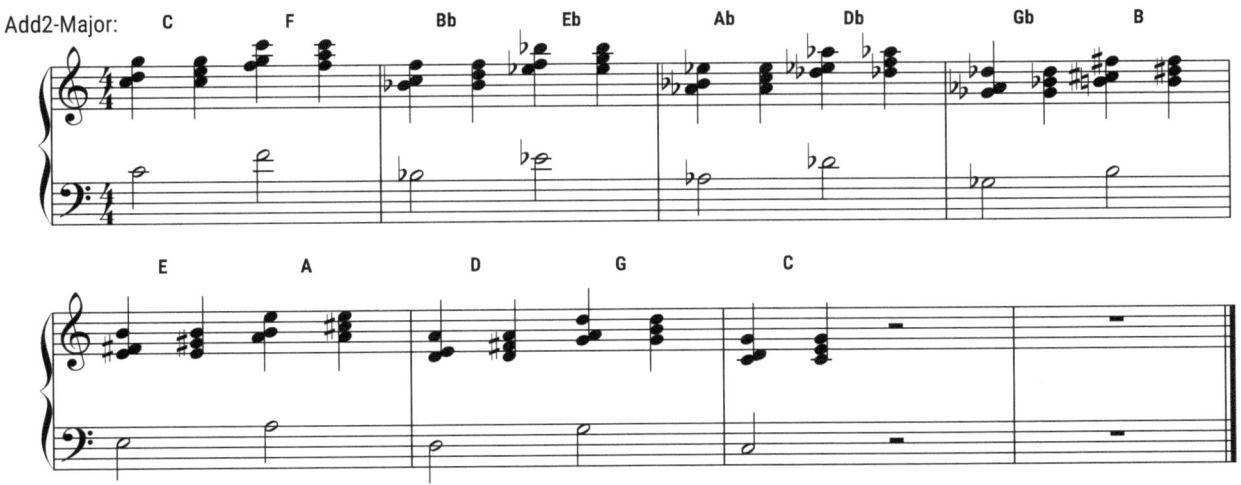

Play the Add2-minor combination in the right hand using 125 changing to 135 fingering.
Play the root pattern in the left hand using 41 or 51 fingering.

Triads with 4ths

Inverting the Sus and Add2 triads

We'll end this chapter with some food for thought by having a brief look at inversions of triads. The full chapter on inversions will explain all of these in more detail. However here we have a chance to introduce the idea of inversions and also learn several other things at the same time. It might be a little challenging, but there is only one basic triad composed of perfect 4ths. It could be fun for you to play with these new shapes and get a different sound. Harmony based on 4ths is called *quartal*. Play through these *inversions* of the Add2 chord. There are 3 notes, so play the 3 combinations of them ascending and descending in the right hand over an open 5th in the left. Use the fingering shown for the right hand and 51 for the left. One *inversion* is a chord based on **4th** intervals.

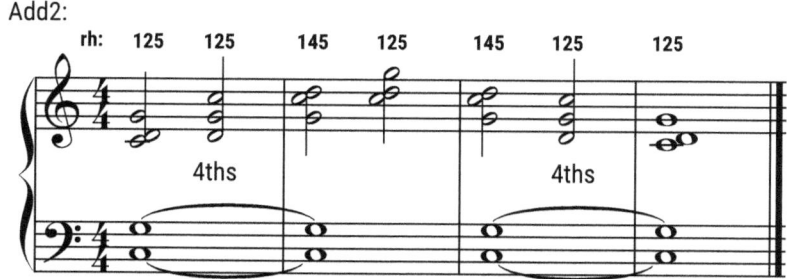

This 4ths voicing has the root, C, on the **top** of the 4ths structure

Now play through these *inversions* of the Sus chord. Play the 3 combinations ascending and descending in the right hand over a open 5th in the left hand. Watch the right hand fingering.

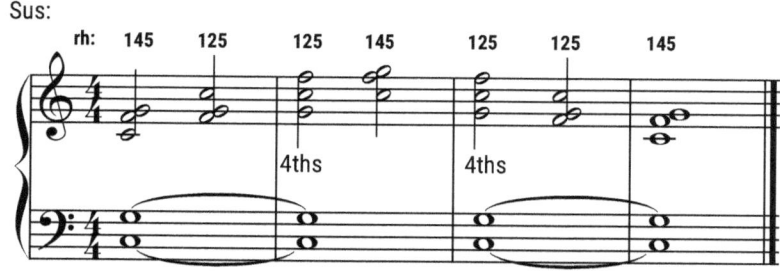

This 4ths voicing has the root, C, in the **middle** of the 4ths structure.

Is there a third way to use a 4ths voicing that has the C on the **bottom**? There are two of them- an inversion of the Bb Add2 or the F Sus. Play through these new shapes in those two keys.

Have some fun playing in other keys. Harmony based on the 4th interval can sound very modern.

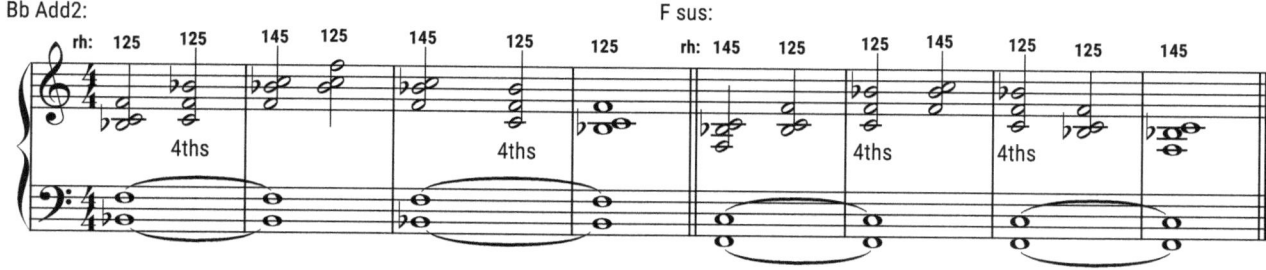

Adding Notes to 4ths Triads

So far we have been learning about the 4 basic triads and that 3 of them fit within the major scale. We have now added a new chord based on the perfect 4th interval. This is already accomplishing a great deal in building a strong musical foundation. When we learn these chords in all the keys there is already a language worthy of exploring deeply. But since we are here now with the triads built on 4ths this could also be a good time to introduce another concept that will be thoroughly covered soon in it's own chapter. The idea of adding another different note to a triad.

There's only one triad that's spelled using just the interval of a perfect 4th. And there really is only one of these shapes for each key. It fits in specific parts of a major scale just like the other triads. We'll look closely at all of those soon. When inverted this 4ths triad can be used in different ways in some other keys as we have now played and heard. We can hear this 4ths triad gives a non defined sound with regard to tonality since there isn't a major or minor 3rd to define that. So we have also played it resolving to a major or minor triad as it often does. But what if we were to add a major or minor 3rd to the 4ths triad itself to bring some tonality? How is that even possible?

We can take this opportunity to encourage a little creativity by having a glimpse at just how many possibilities there are to look forward to as we move ahead on our musical journey. Because this is only scratching the surface of how complex our musical system truly is. So try not to get too overwhelmed or confused with what just one more little note can do. We'll keep it simple for now.

What if we were to add a 4th note to our chord? Let's listen to how that sounds when playing a new note in the left hand under the Add2 triad. Take this through the circle pattern, with both hands now starting at different places on the circle. Listen carefully to these new and complex sounds.

Start with major and then minor 3rds in the left hand. 125 fingering rh and just one finger (or 41 or 51) in lh. Play an Add2 triad over a major 3rd in the left hand. Watch for the enharmonic spellings.

Now play an Add2 triad over a minor 3rd in the left hand. Watch again for enharmonic spellings.

We can explore even more harmonic possibilities with just the 4ths triad and now adding a new note. How about if we try something with inversions and invert the Add2 triad and make it a Sus? We will analyze these chords harmonically soon, so for now just relax and listen to these new combinations of notes and initiate the process of cataloging these sounds for future use. Let your imagination roam.

Start by making a C Add2 and inverting it into G Sus. Think again of a major 3rd from C in the left hand and play it. There is now a minor 3rd interval **between** the hands. The left hand plays this note an octave lower, so that interval is now called a *minor 10th*, although it might be confusing at first to even think of this as a member of the C scale when you are hearing it. Once you see the shape, continue on through the circle using 145 fingering in the right hand and 41 or 51 in the left. Keep the distance between the hands at an interval of a *m10th* through each key and listen carefully.

Now play the G Sus with a minor 3rd interval (from C) in the left hand, again played an octave below the chord. The interval between the hands is now a *Major 10th*. Use the same fingering.

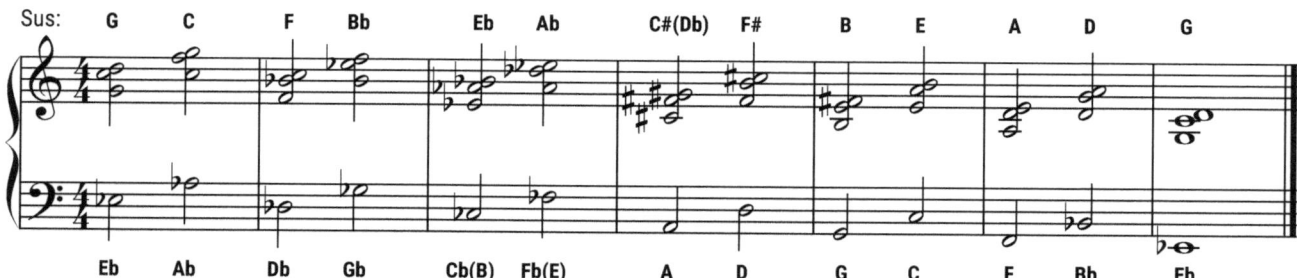

What is your reaction to these new sounds? It's interesting how just a few changes to basic structures can create such different effects and lead to much more harmonic complexity.

There are 12 notes in the chromatic scale. Obviously 3 of them are used forming a basic triad. We have played the 4 basic triads over the root through all the keys on page 62. We could also play the 4 basic triads over the 3rd or 5th of the chord for a newer and perhaps more interesting sound. Try looking again at the chords from page 62 but play them with the 3rd or 5th of the chord in the left hand instead of the root. Listen to how different it sounds with a note from the triad that isn't the root played in the bass. And that still leaves 9 other notes to choose from that aren't members of the triad. Have some fun here experimenting with this idea of another added note to a triad and play some different notes below the chords you have learned so far. Make a list of any you like and when we come back to them we will be able to understand them more clearly, and then organize and further identify them harmonically, greatly developing your ability to use them in your playing.

Making Music Using Chords and Scales

Dissonance and Consonance

Creating and Releasing Musical Tension

Most of us have had the good fortune of reading an excellent story. Or hearing a good joke made even better by the skill in the telling. This narrative quality is developed with a special set of tools. Music is also narrative and can tell a good story that's made even better using the skillset of the composer. Music can of course also have lyrics to add a further way to explore this. But here we will see that music just by itself has a lot of the same principles as other forms of storytelling. The listener intuitively knows this when determining a good melody or musical composition.

When a joke is told, for example, a good comedian will set up the punch line extremely well. Maybe so well that in the hands of some masters the journey to the punch line is the most enjoyable part of the experience. The good joke is well told to the end and the listener laughs. There is a set up and then a resolution. Music works similarly using two distinct forces. One is restless and the other is restful. The journey is **music** and it exists between these two energies working against each other. In the musical world these principles are known as *tension* and *release* and are referred to as *Dissonance* and *Consonance.*

Perhaps the most interesting idea in music is this relationship between tension and release. Indeed a great composer seems to possess an almost magical power when employing this skill. Using it with the element of **timing** within a composition, this skill is often seen as something divine and only understood by a special few with rare talent and ability. It is certainly a rare few that explore the full potential of tension and release.

While the greats remain great for many reasons, the basic skill of employing these powerful musical tools can be conceived of and demonstrated here. That they can be understood is one thing. When listening lo any great music it's very clear that it is also the **refinement** of these skills that define a great work. We often see that the development of these basic principles will take a great composer through their entire creative life, offering infinite exploration to their creative soul and great music along the way. Lucky for us.

There is a wonderful paradox here that is fun to imagine. The idea of *consonance* is relatively easy for us to grasp. It is like home. All is restful. But the concept of *dissonance* is not so easy. So let's try imagining them as two opposing forces at two extremes forever pulling at each other. Restful and restless. Many would think of a long straight line with tension on one end and release on the other, with constant friction between them in various degrees along that line. The forces oppose each other powerfully from each end throughout eternity. Simple to grasp so far. But music will literally stretch that concept. Musically the 'line' is actually better thought of as a rubber band.

Dissonance is the **farthest away** from consonance (home) but the **fastest way back**. The more we stretch the tension between the two forces, the stronger the pull towards *home and rest.*

Dissonant Intervals

The Minor 2nd, Major 7th, and Tritone

We have learned all of the chromatic intervals within the major scale on page 21. As you played through them you may have noticed that they each have a unique characteristic of restfulness or restlessness in various degrees. As you listen and become more familiar with the intervals you will discover that the **minor 2nd** and it's inversion the *major 7th* are extremely dissonant. You will soon identify the *minor 9th* the same way because it's really a minor 2nd played an octave higher. Play these intervals and carefully listen to the restless quality of each one.

The minor 9th is the next chromatic interval above an octave.

The *tritone*, sometimes called a diminished 5th or augmented 4th, is perhaps the most restless interval of all and is used as a component of the **Dominant 7th** chord. We will have a closer look at this new chord next in this chapter. For now observe that the tritone and it's inversion are the same interval because the tritone exactly divides the octave in half. A good way to think of this is to learn that the tritone is composed of 4 1/2 scale degrees of the major scale. The inversion is also the same 4 1/2 scale degrees in a key located a tritone away. In this example we could think of the major keys of C and F# having this relationship. Remember an interval and it's inversion will total 9, so 4 1/2 + 4 1/2 = 9. Another way to think of a tritone interval is to build it with 3 whole tones.

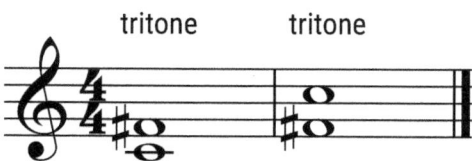

The tritone is located in the major scale between the 4th and 7th scale degrees.
In the key of C Major these are the notes F and B. As you play the tritone from the C scale both ways you'll see that they look different. One looks bigger, but the interval structure is the same.

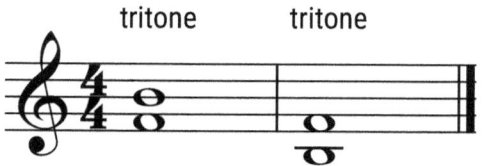

The V7 Chord

The Dominant Seventh Chord

The composer Ludwig van Beethoven will once again provide us with a perfect opportunity. We can play the 'Ode to Joy' theme from the 4th movement of his 9th symphony to demonstrate the use of dissonance and consonance in the hands of a master. We've already played the first part of this theme on page 18. Now play the rest of it and listen carefully to identify the sounds and how these opposing forces are used in great musical works. We can also introduce two new concepts at the same time: *Inversions* and *Seventh Chords*. These two new ideas will be fully explored soon, but they can be given a brief look here thanks to this excellent musical example.

Play the 'Ode To Joy' fragment shown below in 2 different keys. The first example is in C and the second is in the original key of D. It will be clearer to show this first in C and then transpose it to D. Play them and carefully listen to both examples in these 2 different keys and see if you have any preference choosing between them. Remember that D major has 2 sharps (F# and C#). These are shown as accidentals instead of using a key signature to avoid any confusion. We are showing the chord progression in Roman numerals for both examples to illustrate that it is the same in C or D.

First play this in the key of C with the right hand in C position. Use the fingering shown for the left. The left hand plays the G (V) triad *inversion* by lowering the 2 bottom notes but still holding the G. At the V7 in the 4th measure the left hand plays an F instead of a D.
Listen carefully to the difference between the V and V7 chords in each key.

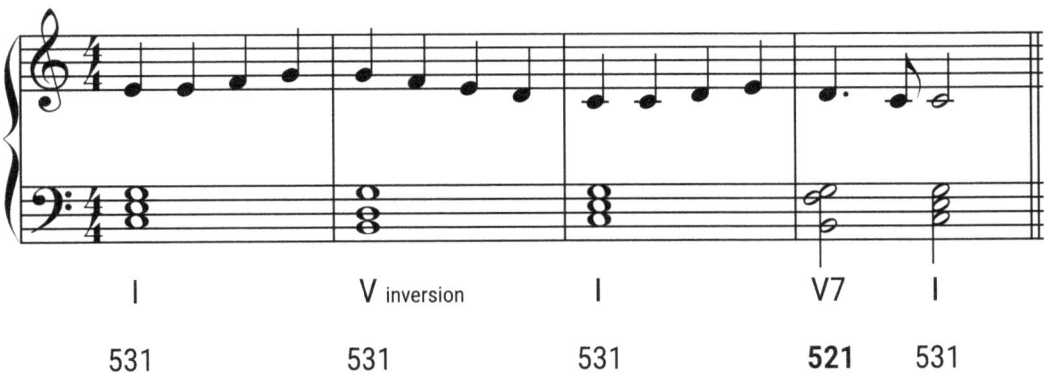

Play the same thing in D- the original key- using the same fingering. Watch for the accidentals.

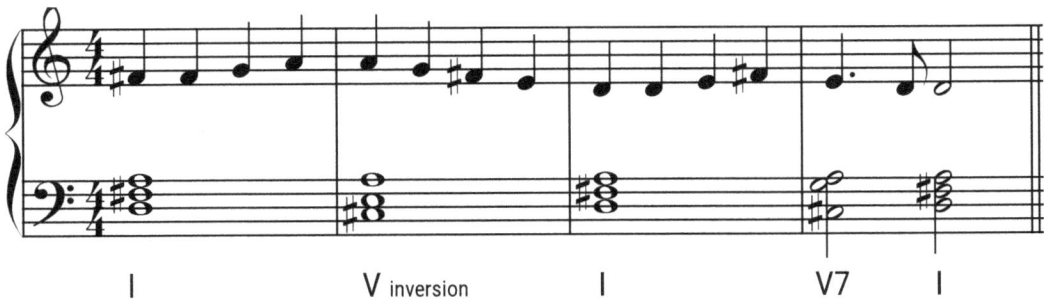

If these shapes are new to you they might be a little confusing, especially if you're trying to understand them harmonically. We'll get to all of the chords and inversions soon. This example can still illustrate the basic idea of inversions and dominant seventh chords at the same time.

The **dominant 7th** chord is called that because it dominates, compelling us to move with a restless quality. In the key of C, try playing just the G (V) inversion and then the G7 (V7) dominant in the left hand. Play each one several times. Do you hear that the G7 has more tension? This is because of the presence of the dissonant tritone interval in the dominant 7th chord. Continue by playing the G chord inversion followed by the C tonic I, then play it substituting the G7 followed by the C.

Left hand:

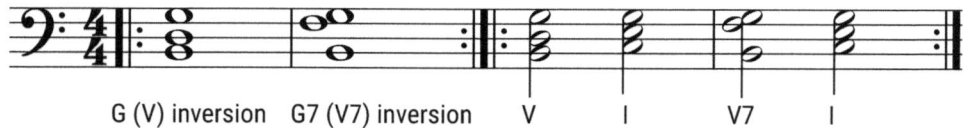

G (V) inversion   G7 (V7) inversion   V   I   V7   I

The tritone is between the **3rd and 7th** of a dominant seventh chord. That's right, the V7 chord has **four** notes- the root, 3rd, 5th, and a **7th**. A G major triad contains the notes G,B, and D. The G7 adds F, a minor 7th interval from the root. This creates a tritone between the notes B and F. Here we are playing the G7 in **1st inversion**, inverting the notes placing the root at the top of the seventh chord.

This V7 inversion is usually played **incomplete without the 5th** of the chord. Here is an instance where less is definitely more, another musical challenge to our conventional thinking. By playing the dominant seventh chord in this inversion and omitting the 5th we expose the tritone without any notes between it. More notes would cause more tonal clutter. Try playing this inversion of the chord again with the 5th and then without the 5th and hear that fewer notes gives it more 'bite'.

Left hand:

G7 (V7)   G7 (V7) 1st inversion   G7 1st inversion   w/o 5th

In our musical example the composer waits by using only the calmer V inversion for most of the theme, saving the much more dissonant V7 until the very last moment before returning to the final tonic I chord at the end. This clever use of tension and release gives the dominant 7th chord it's maximum effect- like the coiling and releasing of a spring- adding momentum at the very end of the theme to drive the music towards home. Play it switching the V or V7 chords and see your reaction. By playing both hands in 5 finger position and then playing a V7 chord in the left hand we are now playing 6 notes of a scale. The 7th scale degree is called the **leading tone**. This refers to it's quality melodically. Listen to a scale played ascending and ending on the 7th. Do you hear how it seems to cause tension by stopping there and then it pulls us to a resolution? It wants to lead us somewhere.

The Modes of the Major Scale

By this point it is obvious that there is a great amount of potential within the major scale. As a source of melody and chords there are so many possibilities. It turns out there is even more potential once we explore the *modes.* Let's look again at the I-vii chord pattern of the scale and now we'll add the names of the seven modes.

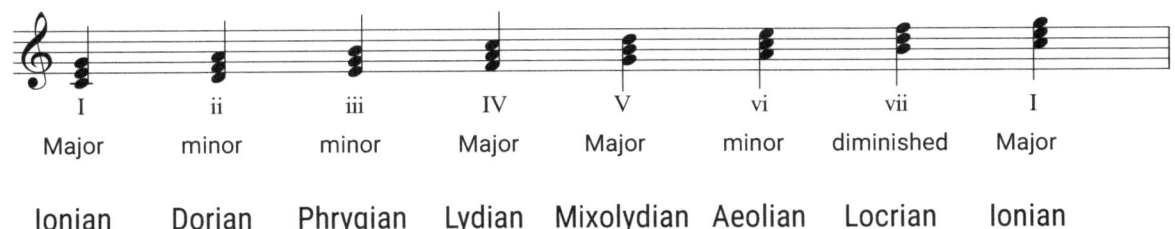

I	ii	iii	IV	V	vi	vii	I
Major	minor	minor	Major	Major	minor	diminished	Major
Ionian	Dorian	Phrygian	Lydian	Mixolydian	Aeolian	Locrian	Ionian

We know that I, IV, and V are major and that ii, iii, and vi are minor. It is the same with the modes. Let's start with listening to the *Dorian mode*, the minor mode based on the 2nd scale degree. First play a C major scale up and down over a D minor chord. Then play the *Dorian mode* over the same D minor chord. Use the same fingering for C and just place your right thumb on D and play an octave up and down from D to D. Listen while you alternate between the two scales over the chord

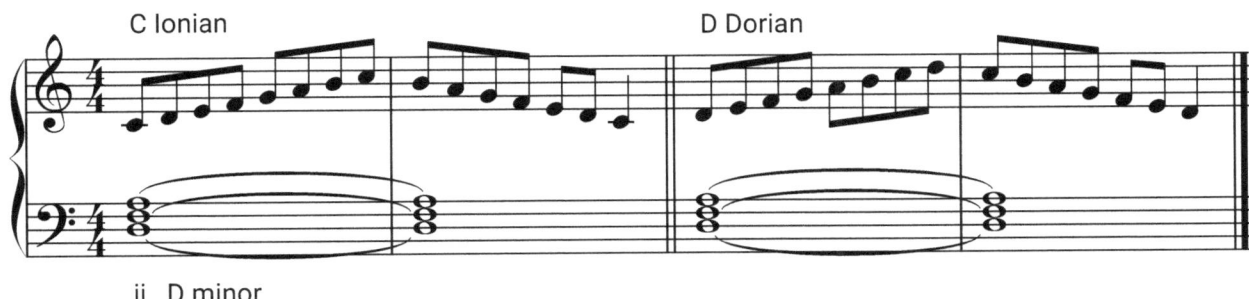

Although it doesn't seem like it should be so different, there clearly is quite a difference in the sound. Let's try listening the other way. Play D Dorian over a C major and then a D minor triad.

It's interesting how the sound is perhaps a little wrong somehow, but not enough to discard it. The idea of the same notes having such an impact when played differently might be hard to grasp. Let's explore this idea musically and use a familiar modal song to demonstrate this concept.

Here is the example we have already played from page 19, now harmonized with some basic chords played in the left hand. Watch how the major and minor harmonies change.

Greensleeves

fingers:

D minor   C Major   D minor   A Major   D minor

These harmonies are all derived from scales and modes. Looking at the right hand we are playing notes from D natural minor, the relative minor scale of F major. This is also known as the mode of the 6th scale degree, the *Aeolian mode* of F. The left hand here plays major and minor chords.

Things change at the seventh measure with an accidental- C sharp- played in both hands. This creates a major harmony on A, making it a V major triad of D minor, the key we are in. Here the A major chord is played in *1st inversion*. Chord inversions are explained in more detail on page 82.

This difference in the scale still outlines D minor but sharps the seventh. This is why this scale is called the *harmonic minor* scale of D minor. Changing the **harmony** of the minor V chord played in natural minor to a major V chord really helps to define the *tonal center* and that drives us home to the tonic, in this case D minor. This is a classic V-i chord progression. As you see there is a C natural played until the very end of the phrase, staying in Aeolian mode. This saves the change in harmony and waits until the end and uses it there to create maximum tension and momentum pulling towards the tonic i minor- D. Now we can see and hear why this tone of C sharp is called the **leading tone** of the D scale. It leads us back to the tonic and rest. This works for tonic I major also.

Play these two different minor scales over a D minor chord and listen carefully to both scales and the pull of the leading tone back to the tonic when using the harmonic minor variant.

D natural minor   D harmonic minor

When playing the Aeolian mode we are playing a scale based on the 6th scale degree of a major scale. Here we are playing D as the Aeolian mode, or relative minor, of the F major scale.
We can also call this scale D natural minor. Sharping the 7th gives us the D harmonic minor scale.
Is there another minor scale or mode we can use on Greensleeves? We'll try on the next page.

Let's adapt the melodic line of Greensleeves to the Dorian mode by playing a B natural in measure three instead of a B flat. This is now playing the Dorian mode of C major until measure seven. What is your reaction to this change? Does it make it sound prettier or more modern to you?

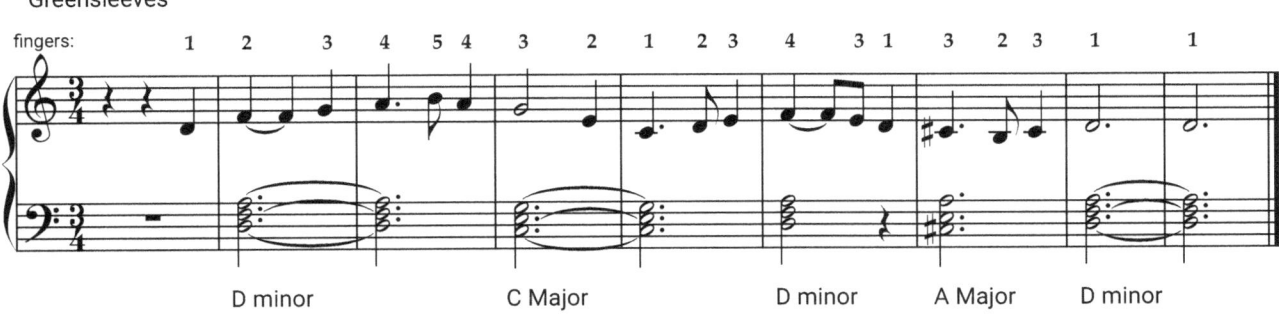

Now play and listen to the D Dorian mode next to the D harmonic minor scale over a D minor chord.

We've established that there are some variations in a minor sound. We've looked at three choices so far- the ii Dorian and vi Aeolian modes, and harmonic minor. There is one more minor scale variant to listen to, the ascending melodic minor scale. We have already played the descending melodic minor scale- it's the same as the natural minor scale.
Now listen closely to the ascending melodic minor scale over the same D minor chord.

Play this exotic sounding scale up and down next to harmonic minor and hear the differences compared to the other minors. We'll be returning to the ascending melodic minor in a later chapter.

Aeolian and Dorian modes are the most used minor modes and the usual sources for a minor scale. Let's look now at the three major modes- built on the I, IV, and V positions of the major scale.

Major modes- Ionian, Lydian, Mixolydian

There are 3 major scale modes at the same positions of the major triads, the I, IV, and V.
The first mode on the tonic is called the *Ionian mode* and we already know it as the major scale.
You can already play the Ionian mode in all 12 keys, hopefully without any difficulties.

Lydian mode is a major mode based on the 4th scale degree. The IV chord is major. If we build a
scale on the 4th degree of C major starting on F, it sounds like F major with a sharp 4th interval.
We are not playing F major, which has a B flat. By playing B natural we are sharping the 4th note.

This means playing **any major scale with a sharp 4th is the Lydian mode** of a particular scale.

First play F Lydian. Then Play C major with a sharp 4th, the Lydian mode of G major. Play it as a G
major scale but starting on C, the 4th scale degree. This is C Lydian, the 4th mode of G major.

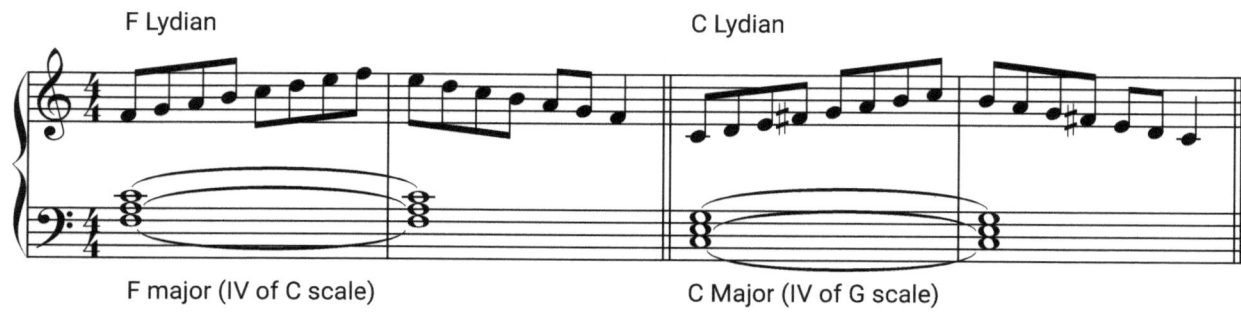

Mixolydian mode is a major mode based on the 5th scale degree. The V chord is major. If we build
a scale on the 5th scale degree of C major starting on G, it sounds like a G major scale with a
flatted 7th interval. We're not playing G major, which has an F sharp. By playing an F natural we are
flatting the 7th note.

This means playing **any major scale with a flat 7th is the Mixolydian mode** of a particular scale.

First play G Mixolydian. Then play C major with a flat 7th, the Mixolydian mode of F major. Play it as
an F major scale starting on C, the 5th scale degree. This is C Mixolydian, the 5th mode of F major

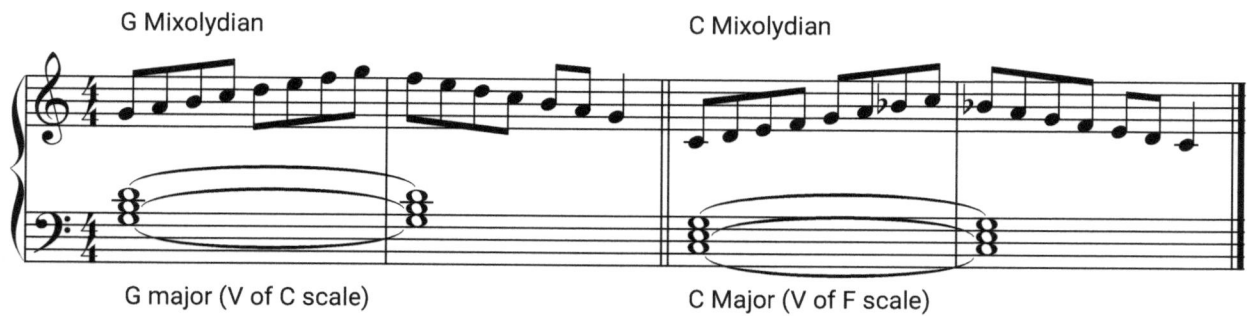

The Phyrgian and Locrian modes

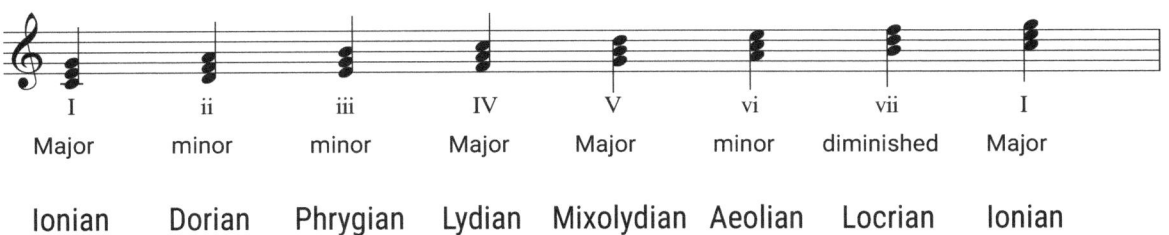

I	ii	iii	IV	V	vi	vii	I
Major	minor	minor	Major	Major	minor	diminished	Major
Ionian	Dorian	Phrygian	Lydian	Mixolydian	Aeolian	Locrian	Ionian

The Phrygian and Locrian modes are the most *dissonant* modes and have a minor sound, although they can be tonally ambiguous. They are built on the 3rd and 7th scale degrees of the major scale.

Phrygian mode is a minor sounding mode built on the 3rd degree of the scale. The iii chord is minor. However here we are going to play a chord composed of a root, 2nd, 4th, and 5th to outline the unusual sound of this mode. By omitting the 3rd we can hear this sound a little differently.
If we build a scale on the 3rd scale degree of C major it sounds like E major with a flatted 2nd, 3rd, 6th, and 7th. The Phrygian mode has some special qualities that will be explained later.
First play E Phrygian over the E note cluster. Then play C major with a flat 2nd, 3rd, 6th, and 7th.
This is C Phrygian, the 3rd mode of Ab major. Play it over the C cluster. Listen to both carefully.

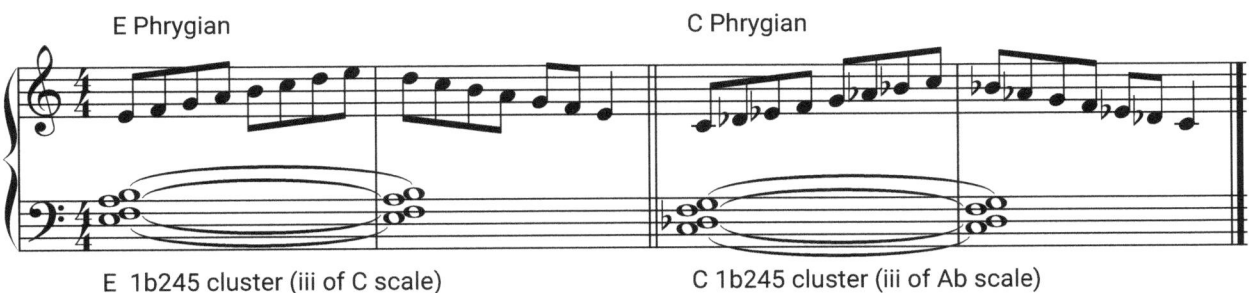

E Phrygian   C Phrygian

E 1b245 cluster (iii of C scale)   C 1b245 cluster (iii of Ab scale)

Locrian mode is a minor sounding mode built on the 7th degree of the scale. The vii chord is diminished. If we build a scale on the 7th scale degree of C major it sounds like B major with a flatted 2nd, 3rd, 5th, 6th, and 7th. The Locrian mode also has some special qualities.
First play B Locrian. Then play C major with a flat 2nd, 3rd, 5th, 6th, and 7th.
This is C Locrian, the 7th mode of Db major. Listen to both carefully.

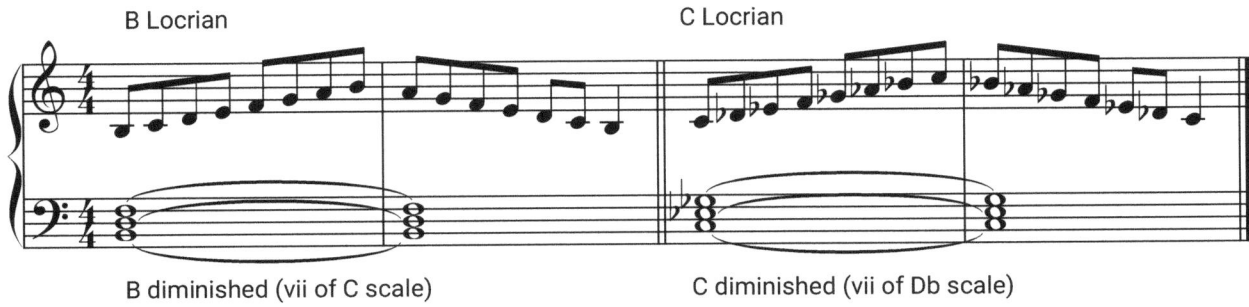

B Locrian   C Locrian

B diminished (vii of C scale)   C diminished (vii of Db scale)

Modes in C Position

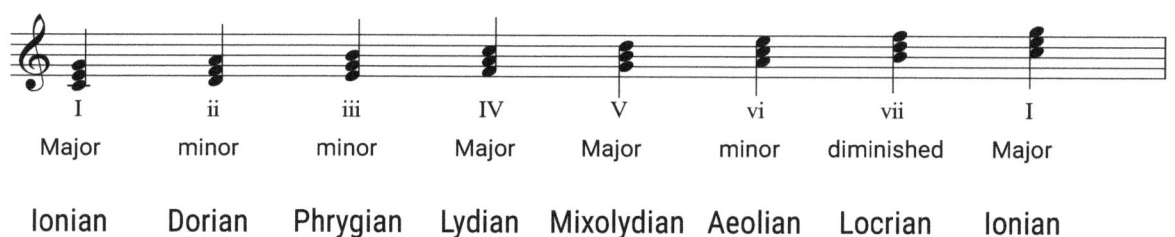

I	ii	iii	IV	V	vi	vii	I
Major	minor	minor	Major	Major	minor	diminished	Major

Ionian   Dorian   Phrygian   Lydian   Mixolydian   Aeolian   Locrian   Ionian

Playing the seven modes in C position is an excellent way to understand them.
We will look at all seven modes as altered major scales and then use those alterations to play the modes in C position. Start with modes based on the scale degrees from C major- D,E,F,G,A, and B.

By applying those changes in C, we can play them as modes from 6 keys- Bb,Ab,G,F,Eb, and Db.
For each mode watch for where the tritone is located and it's scale degrees in that mode.

C *Ionian* has no alterations. It is the same as the major scale.

I Ionian

C *Dorian* has 2 alterations. If we play D major it has 2 sharps. By playing it as the ii Dorian mode of C major we are flatting the 3rd and 7th scale degrees of the D major scale.
Dorian mode is played on the ii position of a major scale.
Any major scale can be altered to *Dorian* mode by flatting the 3rd and 7th. So flat the 3rd and 7th in C and you will have the second mode, C Dorian, the ii position of Bb major.

ii Dorian

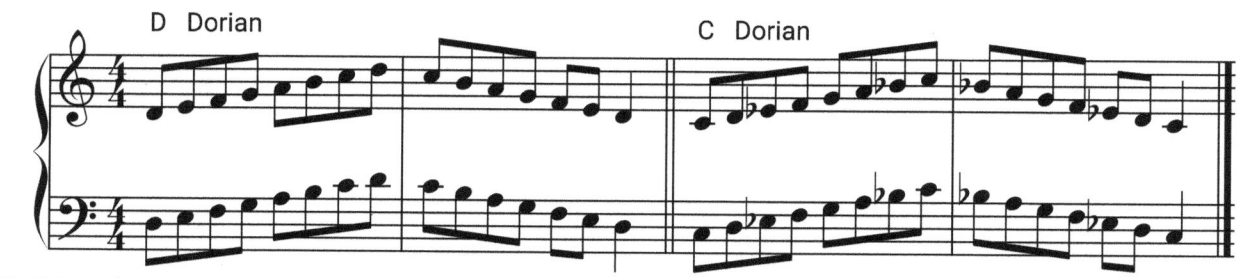

C **Phrygian** has 4 alterations. If we play E major it has 4 sharps. By playing it as the iii Phrygian mode of C we are flatting the 2nd, 3rd, 6th, and 7th scale degrees of E major.

Phrygian mode is played on the iii position of a major scale.

Any major scale can be altered to *Phrygian* **mode by flatting the 2nd, 3rd, 6th, and 7th.** So flat the 2nd, 3rd, 6th, and 7th in C and you will have the third mode, C Phrygian, the iii position of Ab major.

iii Phrygian

C **Lydian** has 1 alteration. If we play F major it has 1 flat. By playing it as the IV Lydian mode of C we are sharping the 4th scale degree of F major.

Lydian mode is played on the IV position of a major scale.

Any major scale can be altered to *Lydian* **mode by sharping the 4th.** So sharp the 4th in C and you will have the fourth mode, C Lydian, the IV position of G major.

IV Lydian

C **Mixolydian** has 1 alteration. If we play G major it has 1 sharp. By playing it as the V Mixolydian mode of C we are flatting the 7th scale degree of G major.

Mixolydian mode is played on the V position of a major scale.

Any major scale can be altered to *Mixolydian* **mode by flatting the 7th.** So flat the 7th in C and you will have the fifth mode, C Mixolydian, the V position of F major.

V Mixolydian

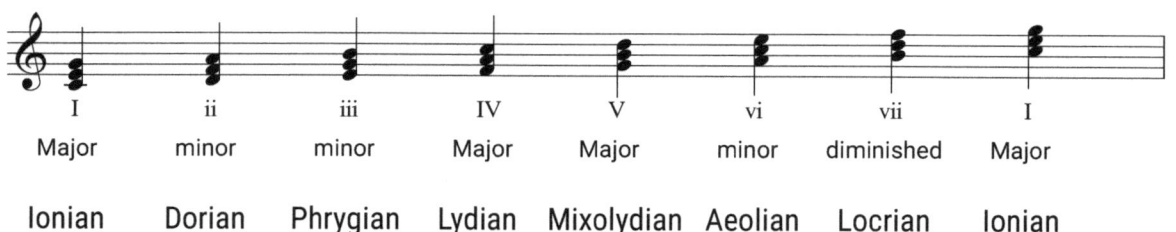

I	ii	iii	IV	V	vi	vii	I
Major	minor	minor	Major	Major	minor	diminished	Major
Ionian	Dorian	Phrygian	Lydian	Mixolydian	Aeolian	Locrian	Ionian

C *Aeolian* has 3 alterations. If we play A major it has 3 sharps. By playing it as the vi Aeolian mode of C we are flatting the 3rd, 6th, and 7th scale degrees of A major.
Aeolian mode is played on the vi position of a major scale.
Any major scale can be altered to *Aeolian* mode by flatting the 3rd, 6th, and 7th. So flat the 3rd, 6th, and 7th in C and you will have the sixth mode, C Aeolian, the vi position of Eb major.

vi Aeolian

C *Locrian* has 5 alterations. If we play B major it has 5 sharps. By playing it as the vii Locrian mode of C we are flatting the 2nd, 3rd, 5th, 6th, and 7th scale degrees of B major.
Locrian mode is played on the vii position of a major scale.
Any major scale can be altered to *Locrian* mode by flatting the 2nd, 3rd, 5th, 6th, and 7th. So flat the 2nd, 3rd, 5th, 6th, and 7th in C and you will have the seventh mode, C Locrian, the vii position of Db major. It might be easier to think of this mode as starting on the seventh scale degree, the leading tone, of a major scale. The first interval in this mode is a minor 2nd.

vii Locrian

Extending Triads

Let's look at the practical limits of basic major and minor triads when used as **extensions**. We can illustrate this concept by stacking triads from the C major scale but starting on D. Bypass the usual thinking by beginning on the 2nd scale degree of the major scale. These chords might be new for you. Start by playing a giant D minor13 chord that begins and ends on D. You'll be playing this as two minor seventh chords, one in each hand. Then play this Dm13 chord as a series of alternating minor and major triads by playing a D minor triad, followed by an F major triad. Continue through this pattern and see the D minor, F major, A minor, C major, E minor, and G major triads. Also see the roots of these triads outlining a pattern of alternating minor and major thirds- D, F, A, C, E, G.

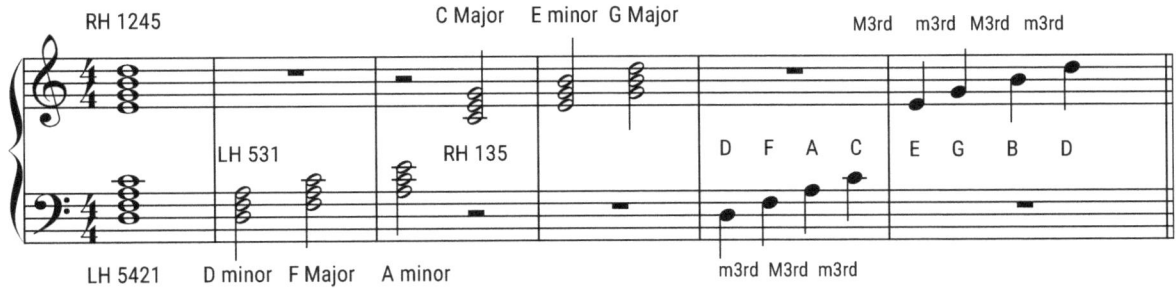

You are playing the root, 3rd, 5th, 7th, 9th, 11th, and 13th of D minor. Here we can play the **Dorian mode** that begins on the 2nd scale degree of any major scale. Play this mode over each of the chords in the left hand alone, **then add D**. What is your reaction to each one with the Dorian mode?

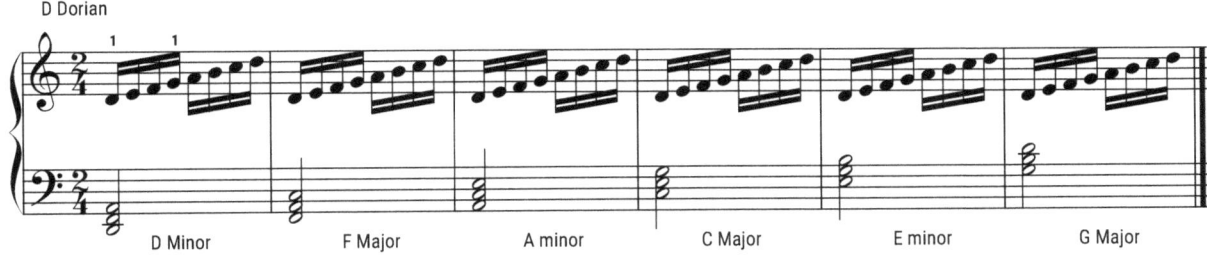

Another good way to think of this mode as an available 'pool' of notes is to see an Em7 on top of a Dm7 with the hands directly over each other. See that you are actually playing all of the notes of the Dorian mode beginning and ending on the note D. We will look closely at seventh chords soon.

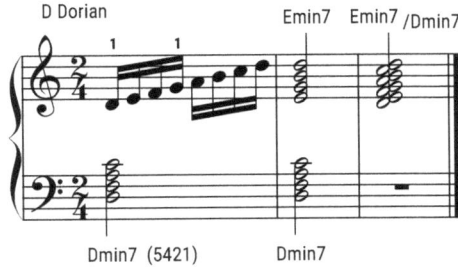

There are modes for each of the seven major scale degrees. To make it easier, try thinking of the seven modes in three distinct categories based on their tonal qualities- minor, major, or 'other'.

Triad Inversions in C

Hands separately

There are three ways to play a triad. Three combinations of the 3 notes. Here are the structures.

	Notes in C Major	Outside interval	Inside intervals
Root position- The root is on the bottom.	CEG	P5th	M3rd m3rd
1st Inversion- the root is at the top	EGC	m6th	m3rd P4th
2nd inversion- the root is in the middle	GCE	M6th	P4th M3rd

There is specific fingering to learn- 125 for the **1st inversion rh** and 521 for the **2nd inversion lh**. We will use the exact same fingerings shown here in C when playing **all** of the triads and inversions in **all 12 keys** and eliminate any changes. Here are some reasons.

If you use the 3rd finger for these inversions it might seem to make sense in C, but it is awkward in some other keys, like B. Also it would leave the weak 4th finger to cover too many notes. Keeping the fingering consistent makes it much easier and faster to learn **all** triads and inversions in the 12 keys as a group. Making as few changes as possible greatly simplifies learning these structures in all of the keys together. The opposite is also true. Changing **any** fingering creates variables and potentially many more probabilities and choices which can lead to more confusion. Keep things as simple as possible for now. It's much better to use the exact same fingerings while learning them all and eliminate any extra moves. Later on you will use any fingering you like. But at this stage it's important that the fingering stays consistent to quickly learn all of the keys together as a group. Play through these combinations in the rh. Use **125** for the 1st inversion. 135 for the other shapes.

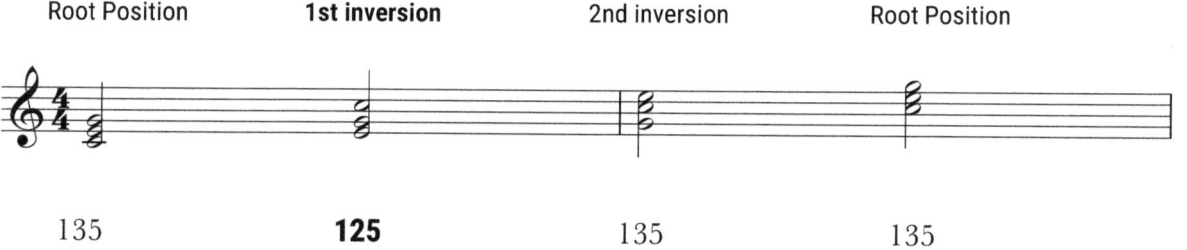

Play through these combinations in the lh. **521** for the 2nd inversion. 531 for the other shapes.

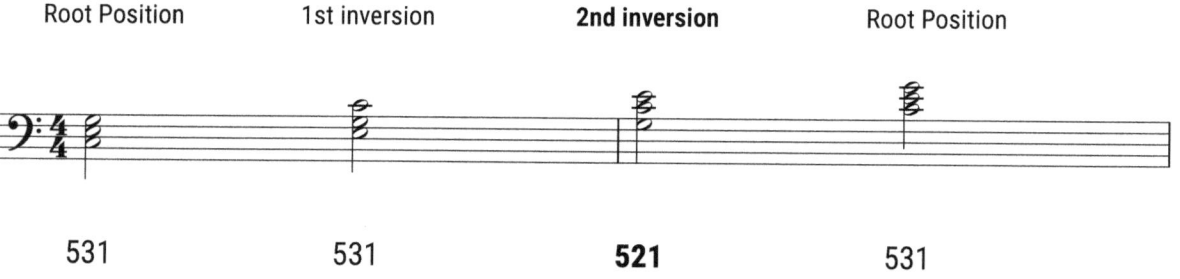

Hands separately- Major and minor

The three notes of the major and minor triads can be played in these three different combinations. The right hand plays them with an important fingering change for the *1st inversion*.

Notes in C Major

Root position- with the root of the triad on the bottom	use 135 fingering	CEG
1st inversion- with the root of the triad on the top	**use 125 fingering**	EGC
2nd inversion- with the root of the triad in the middle	use 135 fingering	GCE

Again it might seem like you could use the 3rd finger for all of the inversions, but that won't work in some other keys, like B. And again that leaves the weak 4th finger to cover too many notes. Keeping the fingering consistent for all 12 keys while making as few changes as possible helps greatly with the process of learning all of them as a group. After that use any fingering you like. Play these in the right hand ascending and descending- watch the change at the 1st inversion.

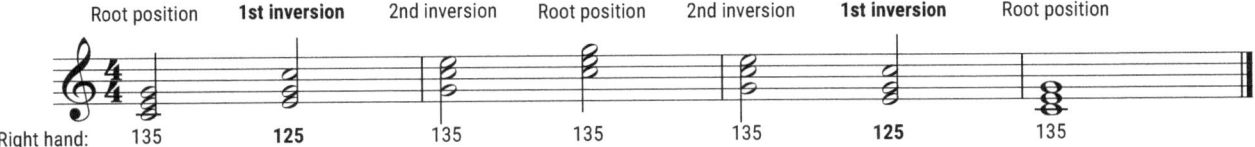

Also now play the c minor triads and inversions in the right hand. Flat the 3rd- E becomes Eb.

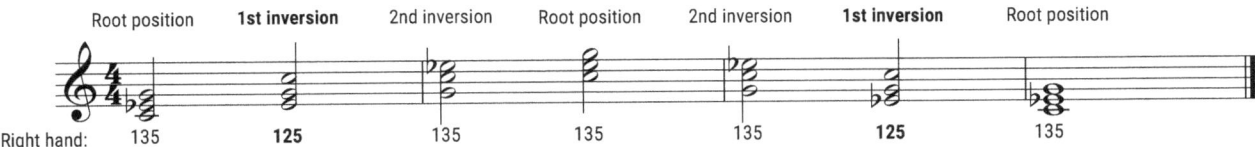

The left hand is different and plays the *2nd inversion* with the change in fingering.

Notes in C Major

Root position- with the root of the triad on the bottom	use 531 fingering	CEG
1st inversion- with the root of the triad on the top	use 531 fingering	EGC
2nd inversion- with the root of the triad in the middle	**use 521 fingering**	GCE

Play these in the left hand ascending and descending- watch the change at the 2nd inversion.

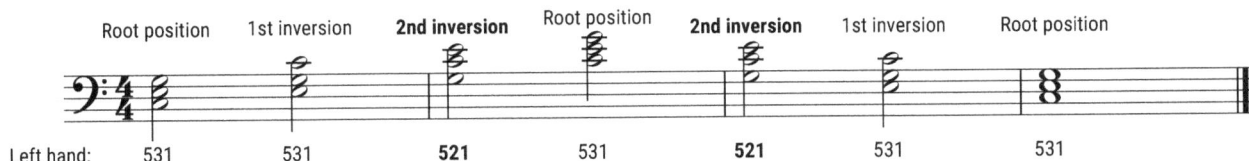

Also now play the c minor triads and inversions in the left hand. Flat the 3rd- E becomes Eb.

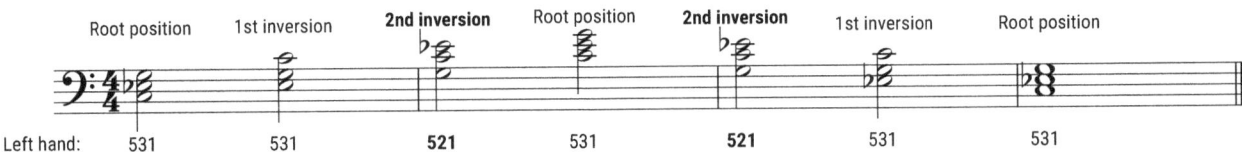

Using Intervals
Creating melodies and harmonies

The next 2 examples use broken intervals in the upper register to create a melody, The intervals in the lower register are played together. When all three notes are played on the first beat of the measure (the **downbeat**) it spells a chord, creating harmony. These examples are written in a time signature of 3/4. Count 3 quarter notes per measure. Play the hands separately and then together. These are easier to understand and play using an approach that's explained on the next page.

Here's the same melody reharmonized with different intervals creating different chords.

This next example is harder to play. It shows the same melody over a **broken chord** pattern that's loosely based on all previous harmonies. Try it slowly in each hand separately, then together.

Chords and melodies work together. Many songs use harmonies that come just from major scales.

These examples show us the value of knowing basic 5 finger positions in any key and how it helps you to play music quickly at the keyboard using fingering. Analyzing the *harmonic movement* reveals that the melody uses only basic I IV and V shapes in the key of C as positions for the hand. As you read the melody in the right hand try to see the intervals and the use of hand positions. Start with the right hand in *C position*- the I (or tonic) of the key. Now play a 3rd and 4th interval for the first three measures. At the last note of measure three move the hand to *G position*- the V of C. Play the same phrase with the same intervals for measures three and four into measure five. This kind of musical repetition is known as a musical *sequence*. The hand is already familiar with it. At the end of measure five the C is played by the 5th finger with the hand moving to *F position*- the IV of C- and staying there to the end. By knowing the I IV and V of the key- in this case C- the melody is much easier to play and all changes of position are understood using only 3 finger numbers. The left hand in the first example plays all intervals using just three positions, D , A, and Bb.

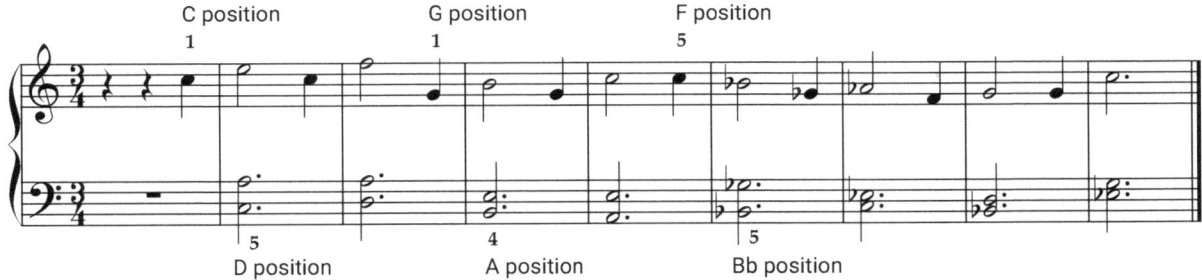

The left hand in the second example plays all intervals using just three positions, C, D, and Db.

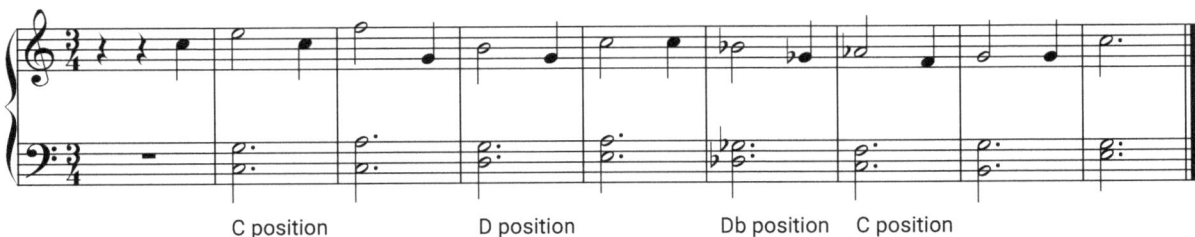

The left hand moves around a bit more in the third example while following a melodic line that uses shapes and sequences. All the fingering is shown. These more complex harmonies outline chords and chord *inversions* from some lesser known keys. Inversions are the subject of the next chapter.

Modes and Chords Together

Play each mode ascending in the right hand over the left hand playing the matching I-vii triad shown. Using C fingering for each mode in the right hand is okay for this if that's easier for you. Listen to all of the sounds and how they work together. Think of each of these chords as a I chord of that particular mode. Some modes (like Phrygian) are often played with a different voicing other than a basic triad, but for now just play a iii minor triad for it- E minor in the C major scale.

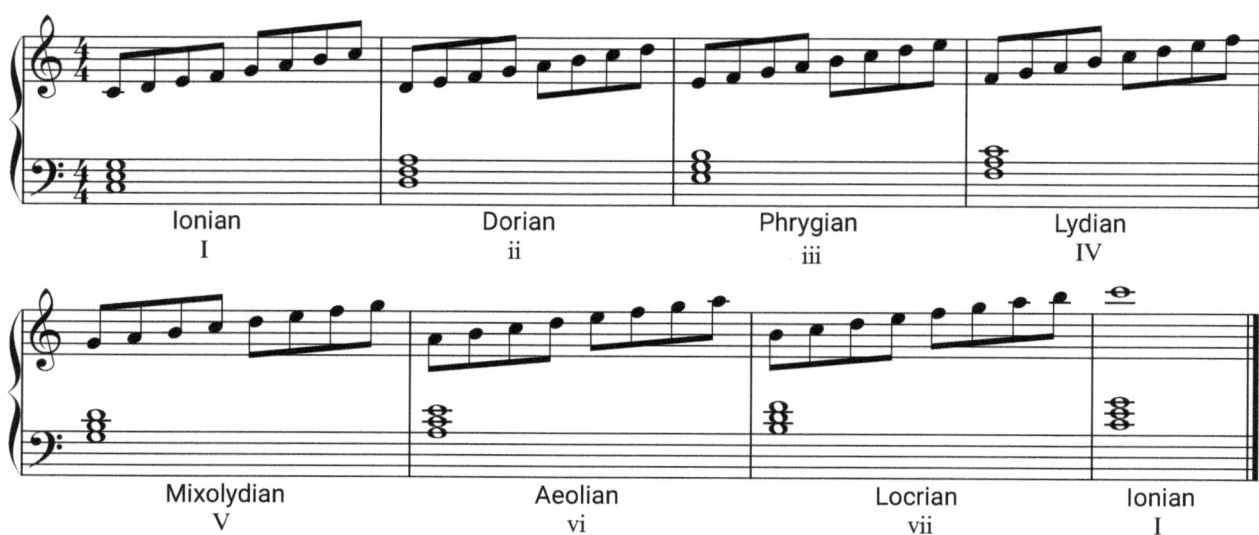

The modes present us with seven very different sounds within the major scale. The major scale is the source of many more sounds than it might seem. At first this might be a hard concept to grasp. How can the same notes in the same order sound so different when starting in a different place is such a simple change to make? The answer lies in where the dissonances are. Watch where they are positioned on the different scale degrees for each mode. As you play each mode, notice where the *tritone* is located within that particular mode. Also observe where the *half steps* are positioned and you will start to see some new things.

For example the Dorian (ii minor) mode has a major 6th interval between the root and 6th, whereas the Aeolian mode (vi minor) has a minor 6th interval. Otherwise they are identical in structure. That would make sense, since D major has 2 sharps and A major has 3 sharps. The difference between the two modes is only one note, but that note makes a real difference in our perception of the minor qualities of each one. Aeolian mode typically sounds a little darker than the prettier Dorian mode just because of where this half step is located. Think of Aeolian mode as minor with a b6.

But how to learn all the modes? There is a way to do that while also working on the major scales and fingering for each key. And also listening to the seven different sounds within all 12 major scales and how they work ascending and descending in actual playing situations. And also work on all of our major scale I-vii triads and inversions in every key. Playing all of this at the same time may seem impossibly far off at this point, but it isn't. We will save energy and time in the end by learning all these pieces separately in C major and then playing them all together the way they are actually used, all while training our ears to hear and recognize these sounds in all 12 keys. Ready?

The key to doing all of this at once is first learning one step at a time. Then we'll put all of them together in C major. After that it will be much easier to move onward through all the other keys.

The first step is to play the modes the same way as in the first example but an octave higher in the right hand to make room for the left, which now plays the I-vii triads in 1st inversion. Use 531 lh.

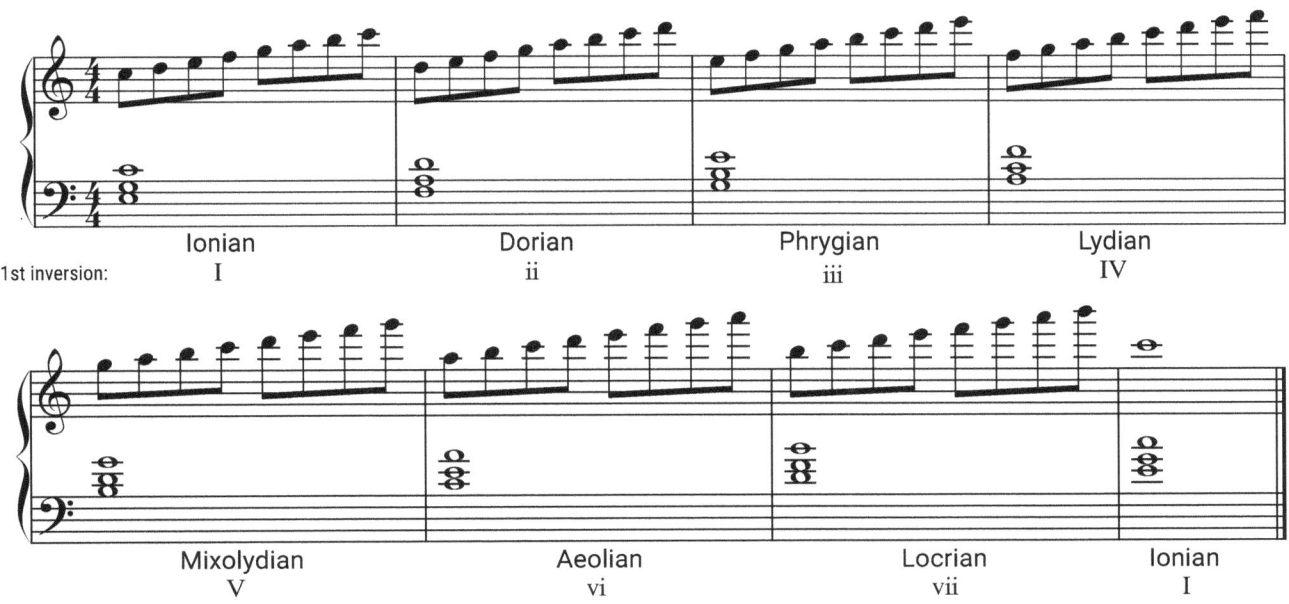

Next play the same thing in the right hand but this time change to the 2nd inversion in the left. Remember the fingering is different for the left hand in 2nd inversion so change it to **521** lh.

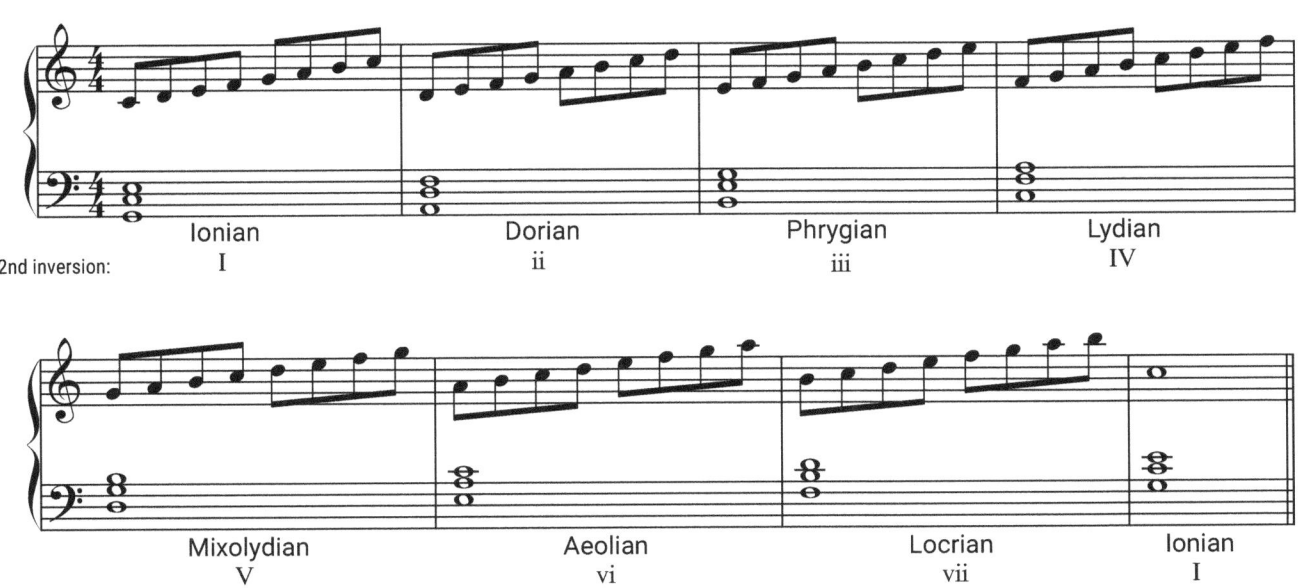

Now play with the right hand moving in the opposite direction. Remember music moves both ways. Play the same idea but *descending* in the right hand. It's ok to use C fingering in the rh for these.

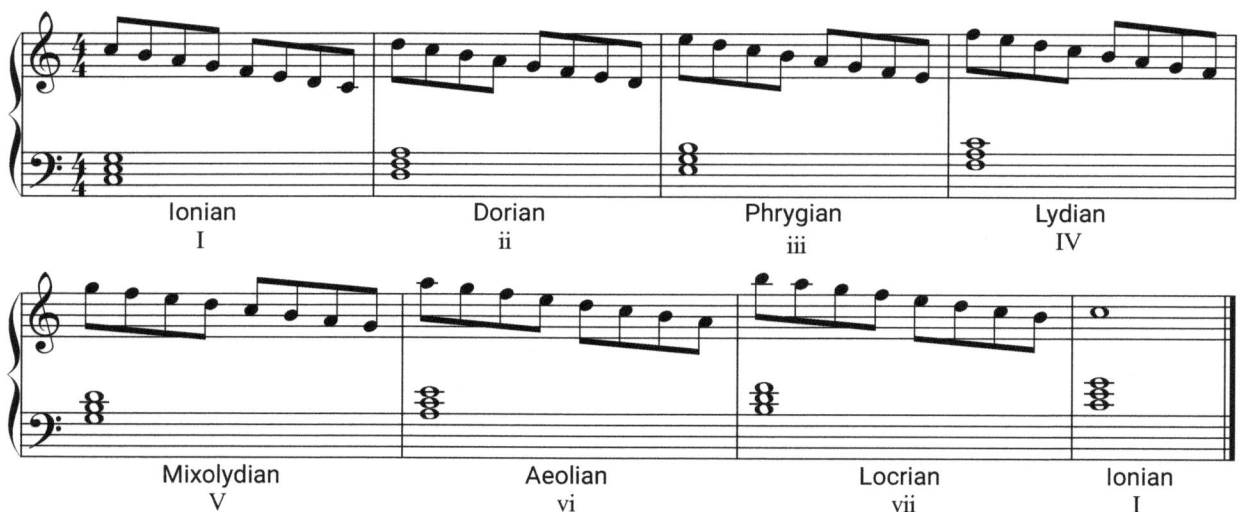

Next play the same thing in the right hand but with the 1st inversion triad in the left hand. The right hand plays an octave higher to make room for the left. Use 531 fingering in lh.

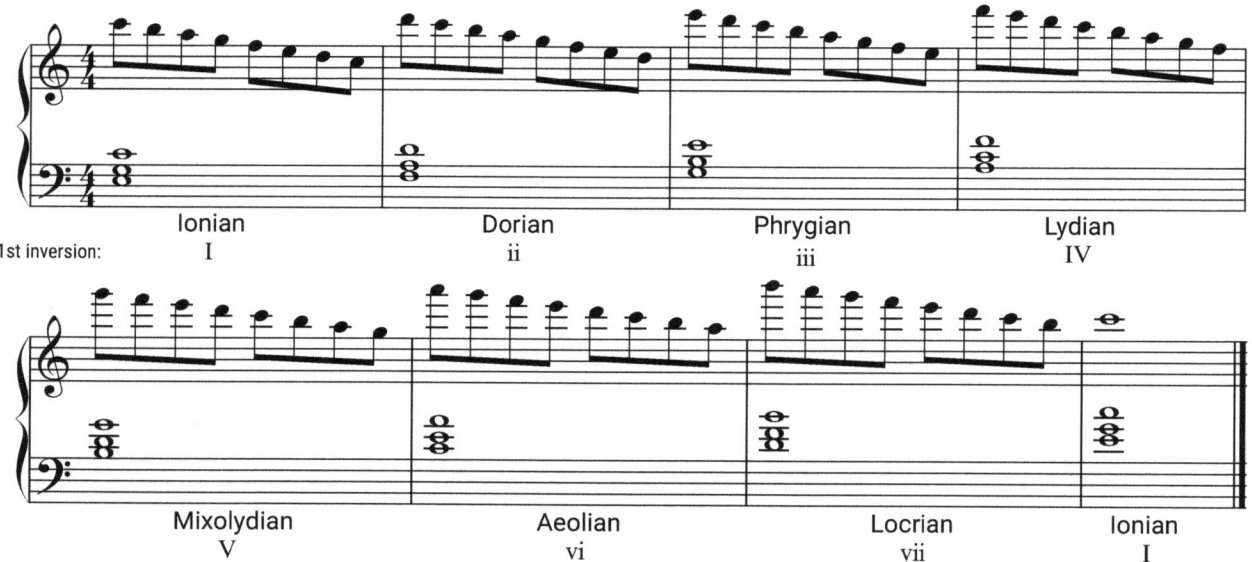

Listen closely to the differences in each of these modes and all the variations. You are moving around by octaves and changing directions in the right hand, and also changing triad inversions in the left. Try to hear the various qualities of the modes and identify them.

Remember the I, IV, and V modes and triads are major.

The ii, iii, and vi modes and triads are minor.

The vii diminished triad and Locrian mode are almost in a category by themselves and sound very dissonant with a perceived minor quality. The vii triad is built using two minor 3rds. Also observe that the Locrian mode has the tritone interval between the root and 5th- outlining the vii triad.

The diminished chord is the only major scale triad with this interval and level of dissonance.

Now play the same thing again in the right hand but playing a 2nd inversion triad in the left. Remember this inversion has different fingering and uses **521** in the lh.

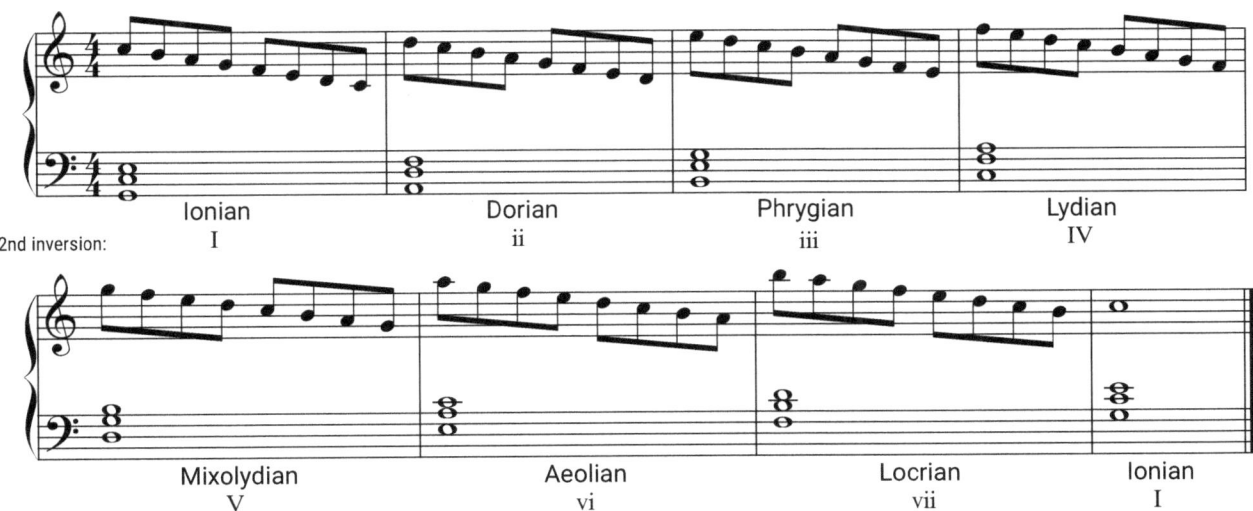

2nd inversion:

| Ionian | Dorian | Phrygian | Lydian |
| I | ii | iii | IV |

| Mixolydian | Aeolian | Locrian | Ionian |
| V | vi | vii | I |

We want to have all of the major scale and major scale triad fingerings worked out to the point of being automatic under our hands. When playing we constantly move in and out of scales from any note in the scale, not just the root. Yet most of us would have difficulty playing some of the major scales starting from any note other than the root, especially using the basic fingering for that scale. It's important for our mind and fingers to connect and be able to not only do this, but also to be able to move between different scales without confusion. The more clarity we have mentally the more quickly and accurately our fingers will move. Here is a way to precisely develop that skill.

We'll start with playing the C scale in a way that also works on modes and fingerings at the same time. As you play through this the first time you might think it's a little excessive to be so strict with the fingering. You might ask yourself, Is it really important to play the F in measure 4 with the thumb? Yes. Don't confuse the hand here. Keep all right hand fingering as indicated. Think of the thumb always on C and F. The scale is seven tones and then it repeats. Think 7 = 3 + 4 or 4 + 3. You are playing two groups of fingers- 123 and 1234. The 4th finger is used only once per octave. Remember that note for each scale. In C the 4th finger plays B, the leading tone of the scale.

The pattern is ascending one measure and then descending the next, each time playing the mode strictly using only C scale fingering. Alternate directions as you play each mode over it's I chord. Play through this carefully and watch for the indicated fingering. It might be a little tricky at first.

Start slowly and play all of the notes accurately with equal sound and speed. When comfortable with the motions gradually increase the speed staying even and equally playing each note. Work on being consistent. Practice your critical listening and concentrate. A good rule is to play it perfectly at whatever speed that is. Usually this means starting slowly and accurately.
It's important to train the hand to be able to take off and land from anywhere in the scale. Here is where the C scale might be a little confusing because it is all white keys. Pay attention. Take your time listening to all of the different sounds and in developing the process of identifying them.

Working on scales and modes at the same time

 Now we can really speed up our progress and gain some practical technique while developing our listening. Do as many things as you can at once to make your time and effort much more efficient. Play through the ascending/descending pattern in the right hand over I-vii triads in root position. Follow the exact fingering shown. The 4th finger of the right hand plays B. Use 531 fingering in lh.

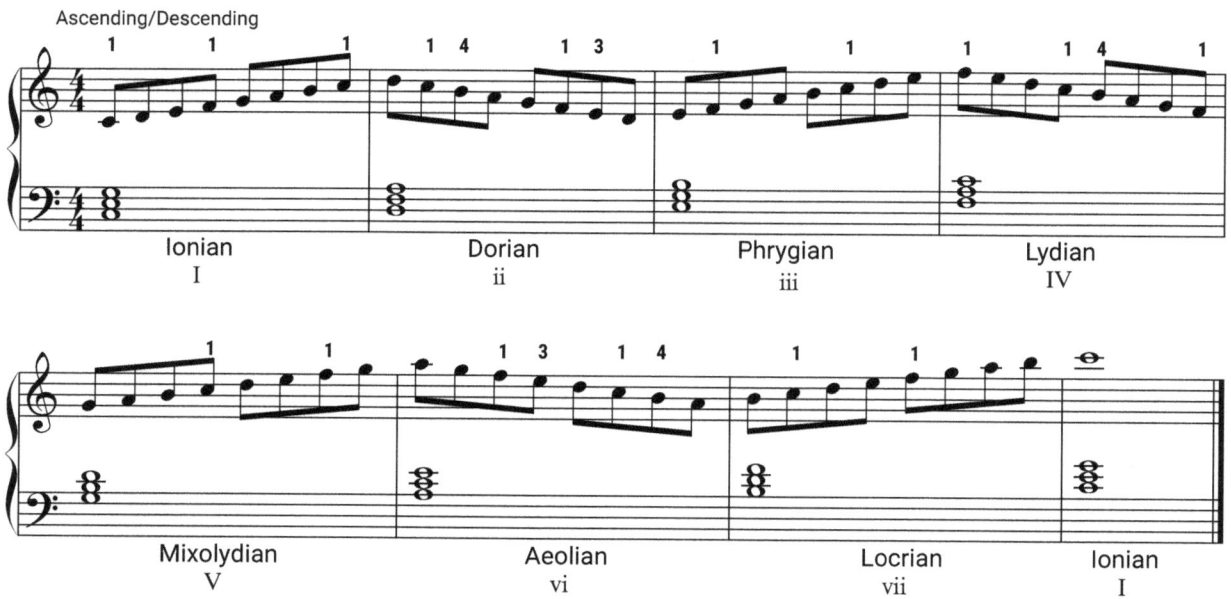

So now play it going the other way to cover the modes in the other direction- start by descending and then ascending. Same right hand fingering with the 4th finger on B. Use 531 fingering in lh.

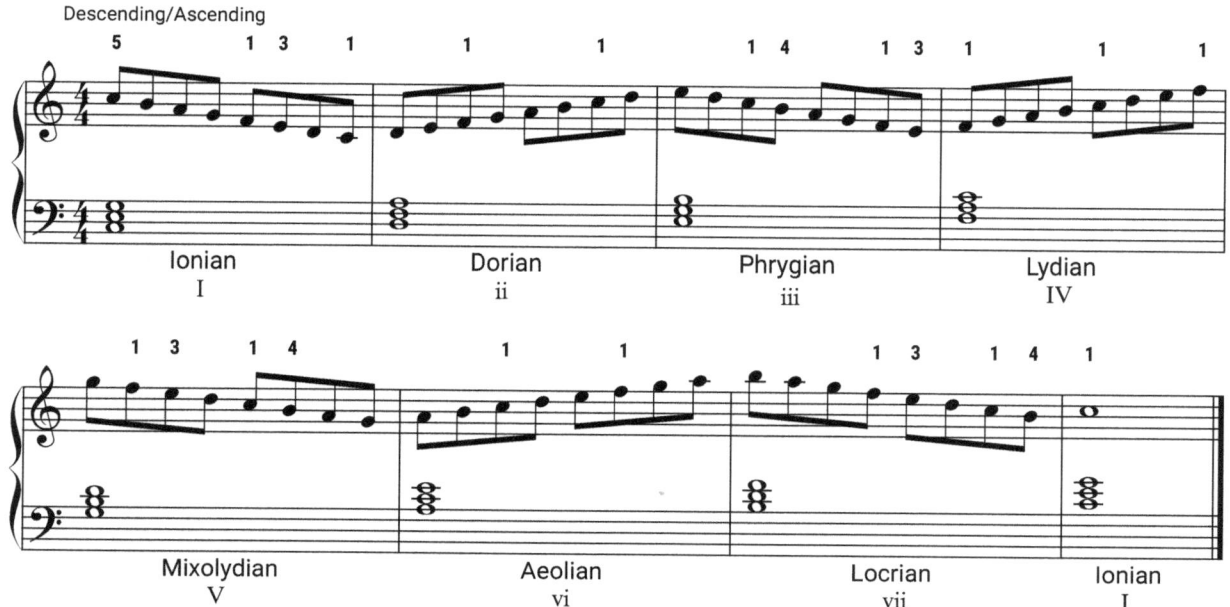

Continuing this process, we can gain even more rapid development by adding another layer to our routine. Now play the same thing with the left hand chords in 1st inversion and an octave lower.

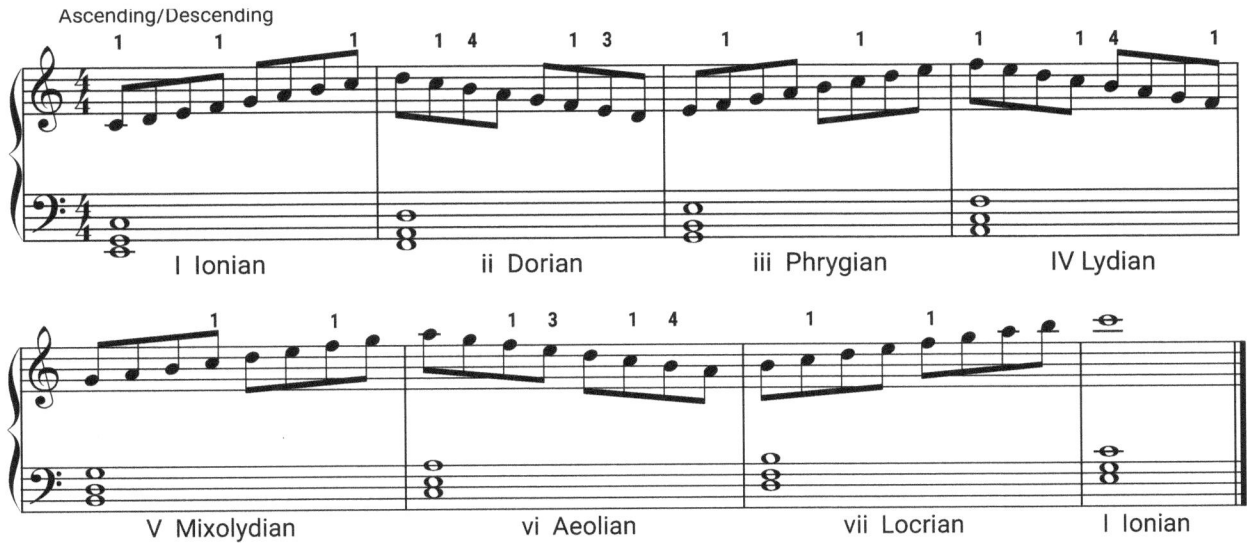

And the other way.

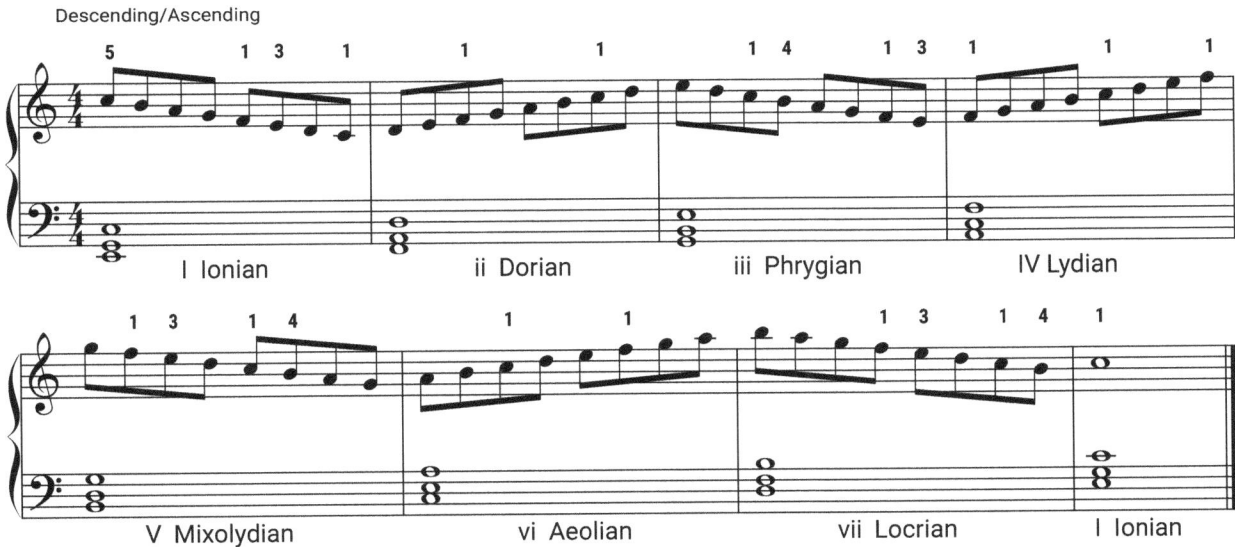

As you play, listen to how different the modes sound when the triads are played as inversions. We will soon see how chords connect to each other using their **next closest** inversions. This is known as *close voicing* or *voice leading*. It usually sounds very clunky to only play chords in their basic *root position*, with the root at the bottom of the chord. The sounds of chords connecting to each other using inversions is the basis for a language that also includes different notes played in the bass. Triads played over notes other than the ones in the chord form a sophisticated harmonic vocabulary that takes this basic concept and uses it to create some very complex sounds.

Finish this group by playing the same thing with the triads in 2nd inversion.
Remember that the left hand uses the different 521 fingering for this shape.

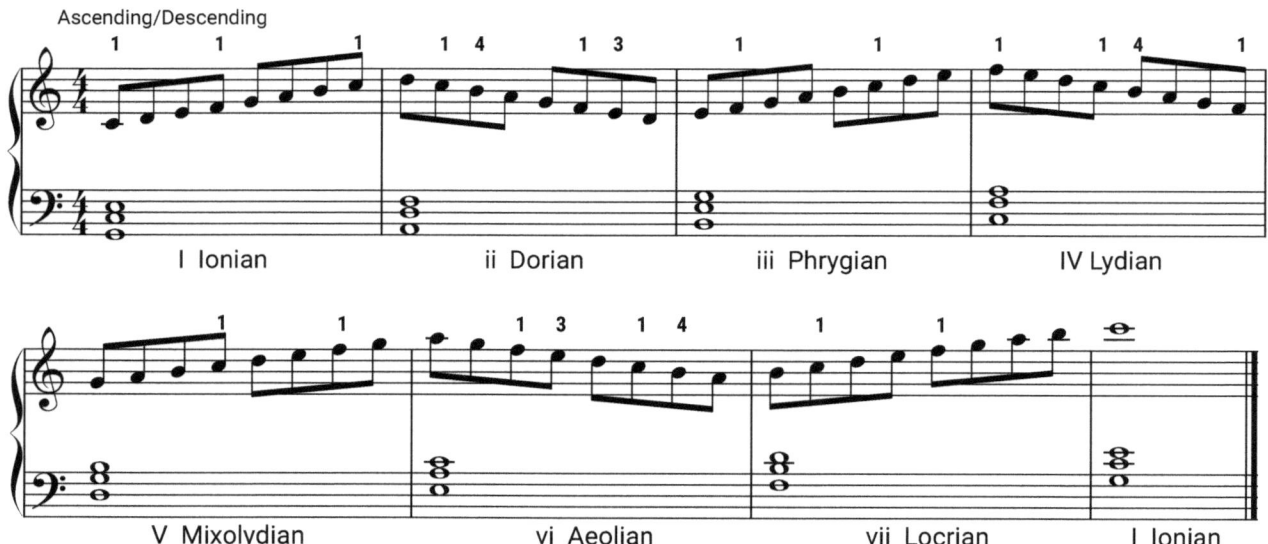

And the reverse.

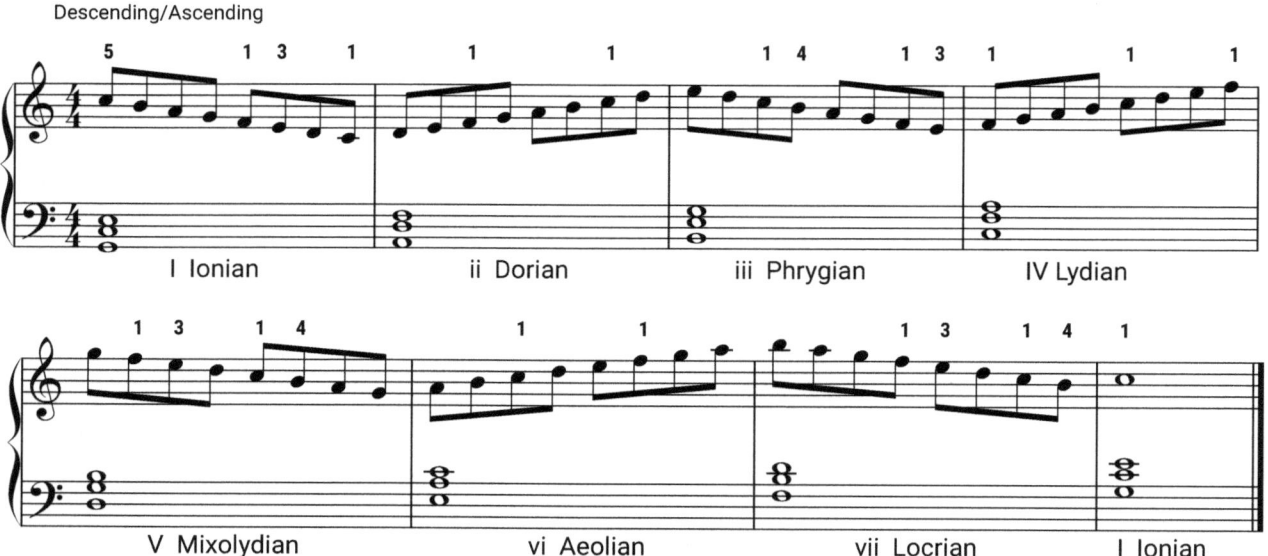

Hopefully by the end of this chapter we have opened up a few of the many possibilities that exist for creating music using a language created solely from the 4 basic triads and 4 basic scales. You will soon be recognizing *tonality* when listening to music and that often what we think are different chords actually belong to a single key. Next we will add another layer to this language using chord inversions and connecting them with close voicing. This is the stage where your playing sounds more mature and developed. Close voicing, or voice leading, will allow many new choices between harmonies and sound very pleasing, avoiding the 'root bound' sound of playing only block chords.

Triads and Inversions
Song Form and Narrative

Traditional harmony defines three basic categories in music- *Tonic*, *Sub Dominant*, and *Dominant*. One could think of the tonic as rest and the dominant as restless, with the sub dominant as the journey between the two forces of consonance and dissonance.
Usually one journeys and arrives at the dominant force that will then spring us towards home.

Remember music exists in **time** and that the best music tells a story with forward momentum. This narrative quality usually forms an internal cycle that can repeat endlessly: tonic, sub dominant, dominant, tonic, etc. and it can take many twists and turns depending on the skill of the composer. But the basic characteristics will be restful, restless, and the journey somewhere in between.

Here we can illustrate these three basic forces as the three **major** chords within a key. These relationships exist in many forms of music such as the blues or folk forms and popular music. The I, IV, and V chords are often used as positions that strongly define a key or tonal center. This example is in D major. The I, IV, and V, chords are the D, G, and A major triads.

We'll use a classic cowboy song 'The Red River Valley' to show how the tonic I chord is home, the sub dominant IV chord is the journey, and the V and V7 are the tension towards release.
Roman numerals are given here to show the harmonic progression. Think I, IV, and V of D major.

Basic right hand fingering is shown. The left hand plays 531 except the IV uses 521 fingering.

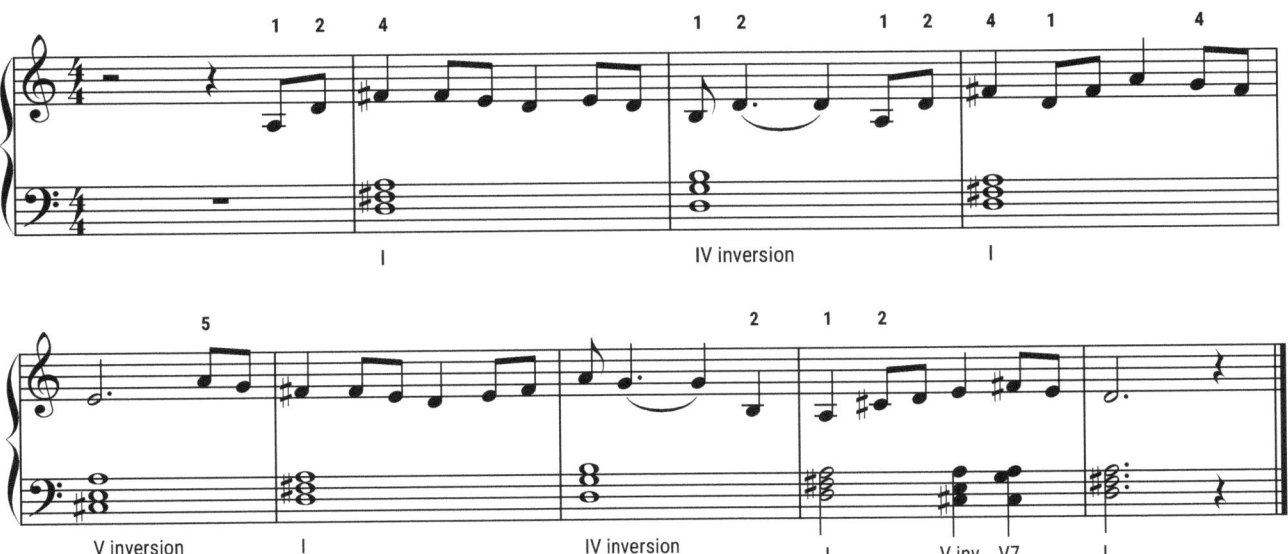

Obviously this simple chord pattern can be modified, especially since the hands are crossing over or even playing some of the same notes. Feel free to create your own arrangement for the left hand harmonies. Try playing broken chords, root/chord combinations, or different inversions.

Triad Inversions and The Perfect Cadence

Using inversions to connect basic chords

We've seen how strong the connection is between the three major triads of the major scale. The I, IV, and V chords are traditionally studied using the example of the *perfect cadence*, There are also several other *cadences* to look at. We'll begin with the one used in music constantly. The I, IV, and V positions have a very strong relationship within a key. One powerful reason is that on the overtone series the first interval after the octave is a 5th and the next interval after that is a 4th.

The *perfect cadence* connects the V chord of a key to the I chord within that same key. If we were to take the C scale as an example, C is the I chord and F and G are the IV and V chords within the C scale. C is also the V of F (as I). They are all neighbors on the **circle of 5ths**. If we look at C at 12 o'clock on the circle we see the F is directly on the left side of C at 11 o'clock and G is directly on the right side of C at 1 o'clock. Looking at our keyboard we can see that the F and G notes are either an interval of a 4th or a 5th away from C moving up or down. The 4th and 5th intervals are inversions of each other, so sometimes the circle of 5ths is also called the circle of 4ths.

There are three ways to connect the C chord to the F and G chords using inversions. The chord progression of I IV I V I will connect the I chord to a IV or V chord using the next closest inversions of those chords and any **common tones** between the chords to connect them.
A C chord contains the notes CEG.
An F chord contains the notes FAC. C is a *common tone* with the root of a C chord.
A G chord contains the notes GBD. G is a *common tone* with the 5th of a C chord.

Using common tones and inversions to connect chords is called *voice leading* (or *close voicing*).

Playing a C major chord to an F or G major chord in root position sounds a little clunky like this:

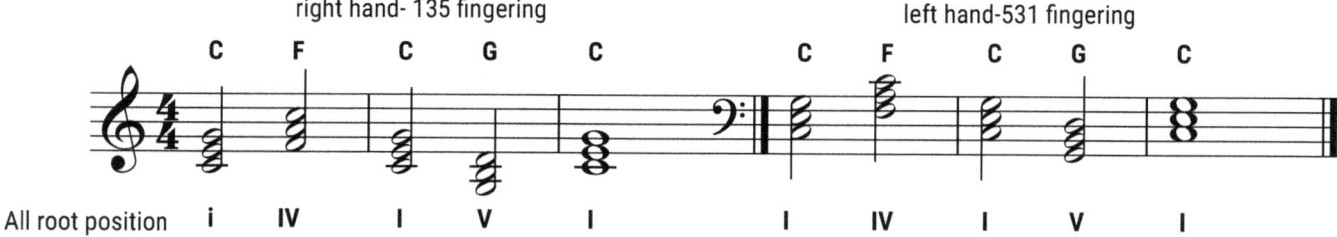

If we play from the root position C chord to *inversions* of the other 2 chords it sounds like this:
Listen to how much smoother the connection between the chords is. Watch fingering both hands.

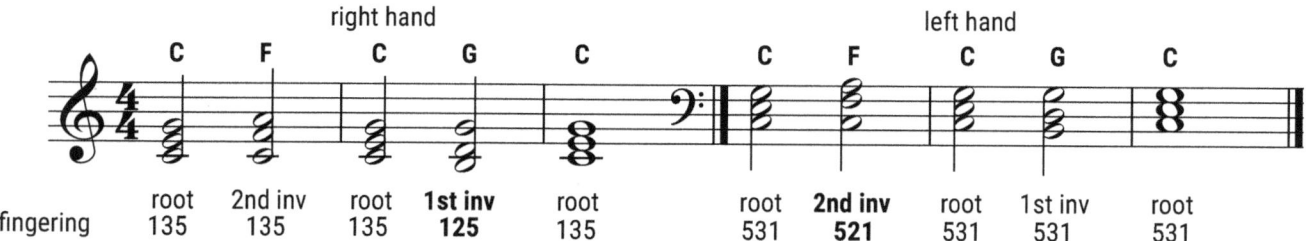

In order to play all 3 combinations of this progression in C we should first play the root positions and inversions of the 3 major chords from group one- C, F, and G- the I, IV, and V of C.
Play these triads with the hands separately and then together, ascending and descending.

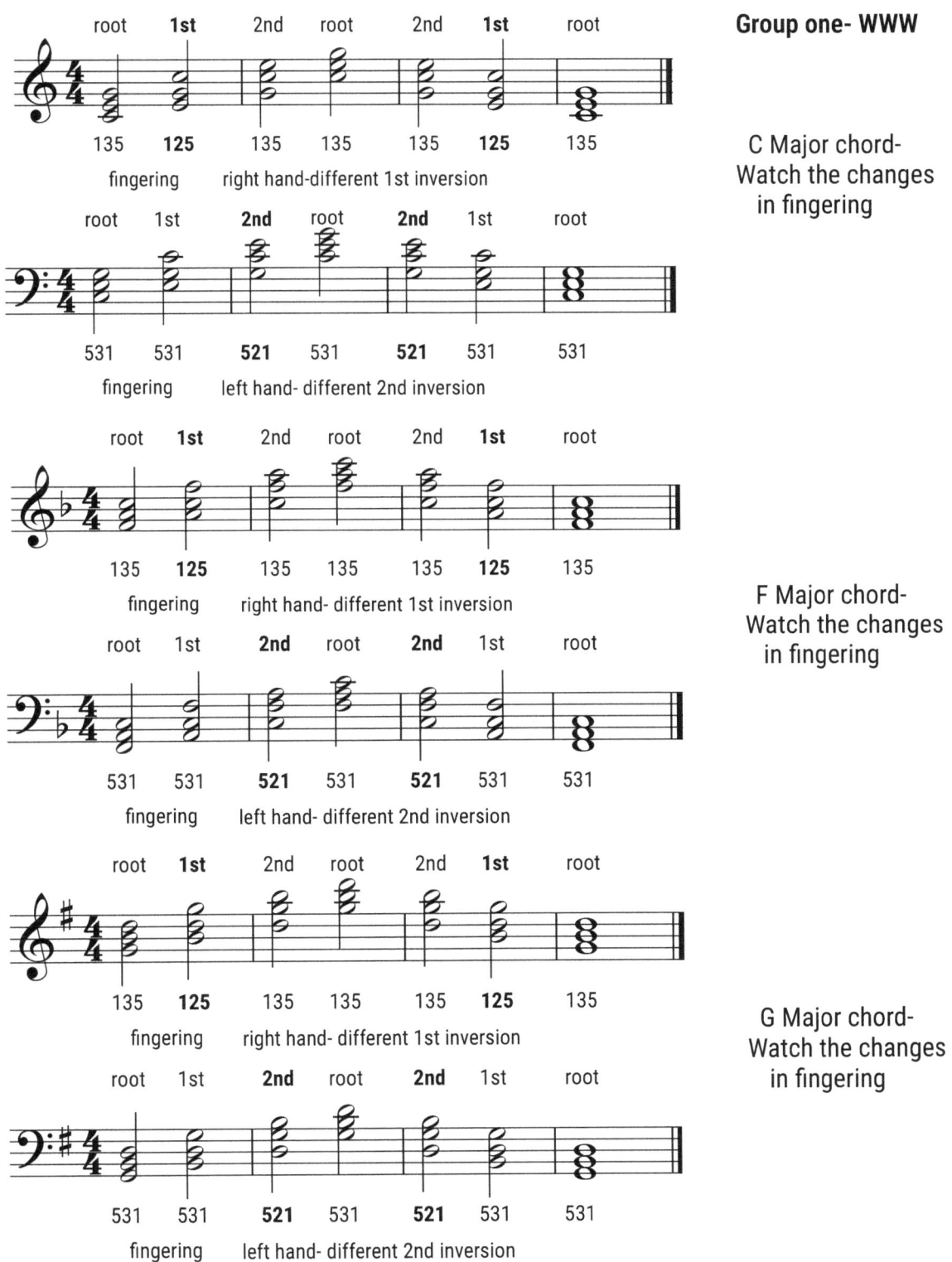

Group one- WWW

C Major chord-
Watch the changes
in fingering

F Major chord-
Watch the changes
in fingering

G Major chord-
Watch the changes
in fingering

Cadence Inversions in C

Now that we have played through all three combinations of the C, F, and G major chords it will be much easier to see all of these shapes together as a group and then to connect them smoothly.

This is the same I IV I V I *chord progression* but here it begins on the 1st or 2nd inversions of the C major triad. It still ends with a V to I. Play in each hand watching for specific fingering changes.

Right hand uses 125 for *1st inversion*. Left hand uses 521 for *2nd inversion*.

Starting with 1st inversion C major:

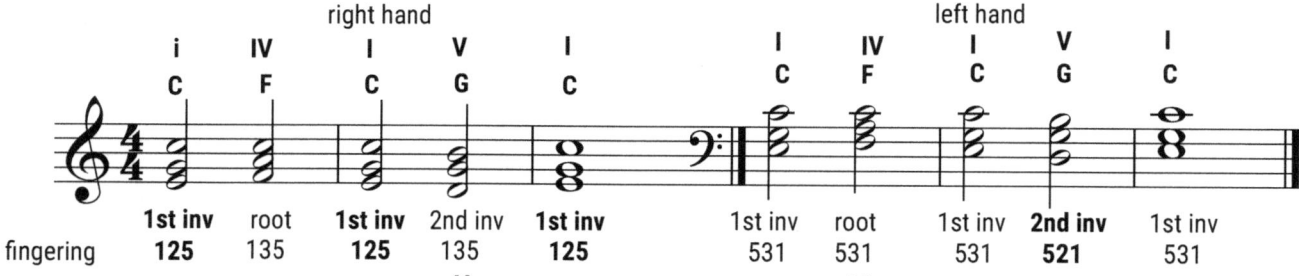

Starting with 2nd inversion C major:

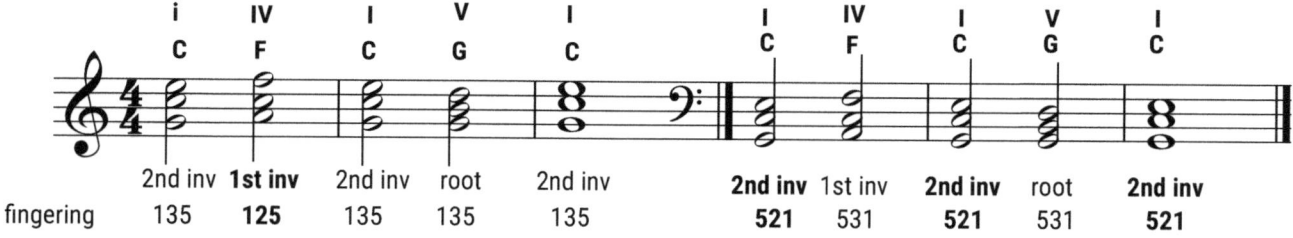

When this feels comfortable play them with the hands together. Watch for all fingering changes. They occur in different places with the hands playing together. The root position is the only shape that's played with the same fingering- 135 or 531- in both hands at the same time.

You see now that it would have been much harder to play all of these connecting chords together without first understanding all of the root positions and inversions for each chord separately. The way chords connect isn't always with common tones, but the smoothest sound is to use inversions, often the closest one. It's important to have them under your fingers. Soon we'll study triads as extensions and the harmonies that are possible. To use other notes as roots is a secondary language. Things are much more complex and part of the reason is using such a strong language in a different place than the usual gives the familiar patterns a surprising new element that's very pleasing to the mind and ears. But that would be impossible to conceive of without playing all of the combinations in all keys beforehand. Although it may seem a bit laborious to play in all 12 keys, we'll soon see there is a way to speed things up quite a bit after developing this first crucial step.

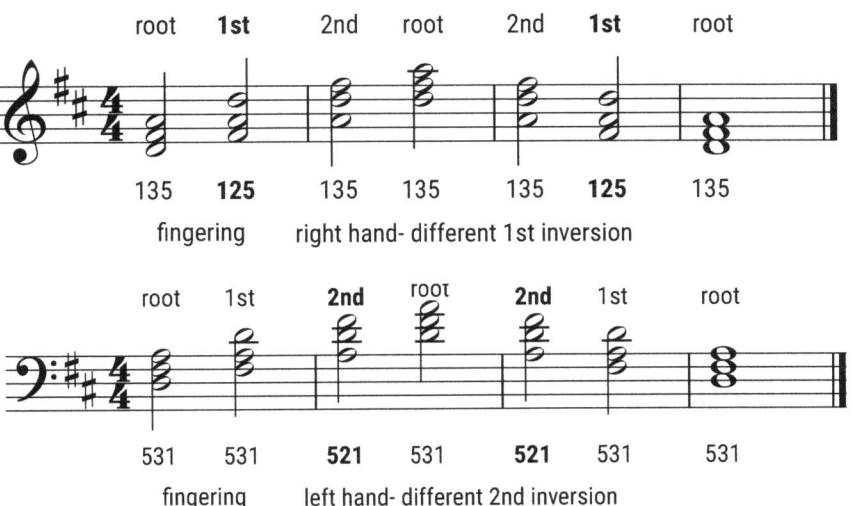

Group two- WBW

D Major chord-
Watch the changes
in fingering

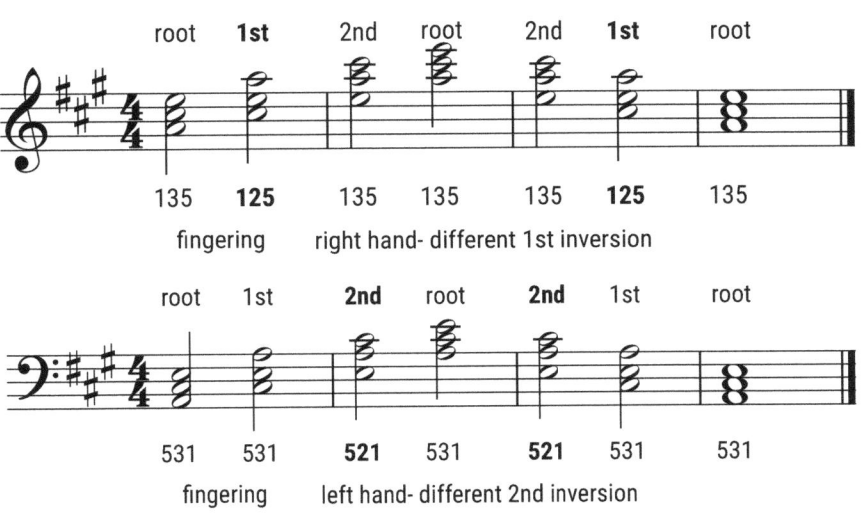

A Major chord-
Watch the changes
in fingering

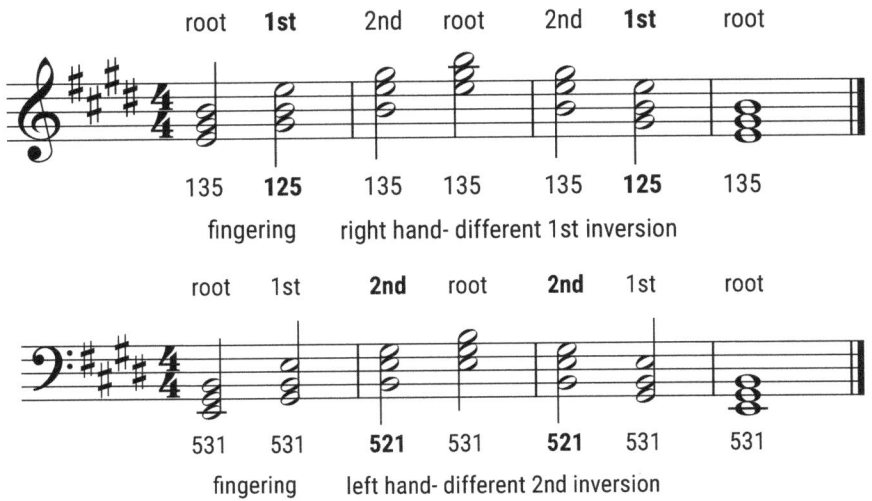

E Major chord-
Watch the changes
in fingering

Group three- BWB

Eb Major chord-
Watch the changes
in fingering

Ab Major chord-
Watch the changes
in fingering

Db Major chord-
Watch the changes
in fingering

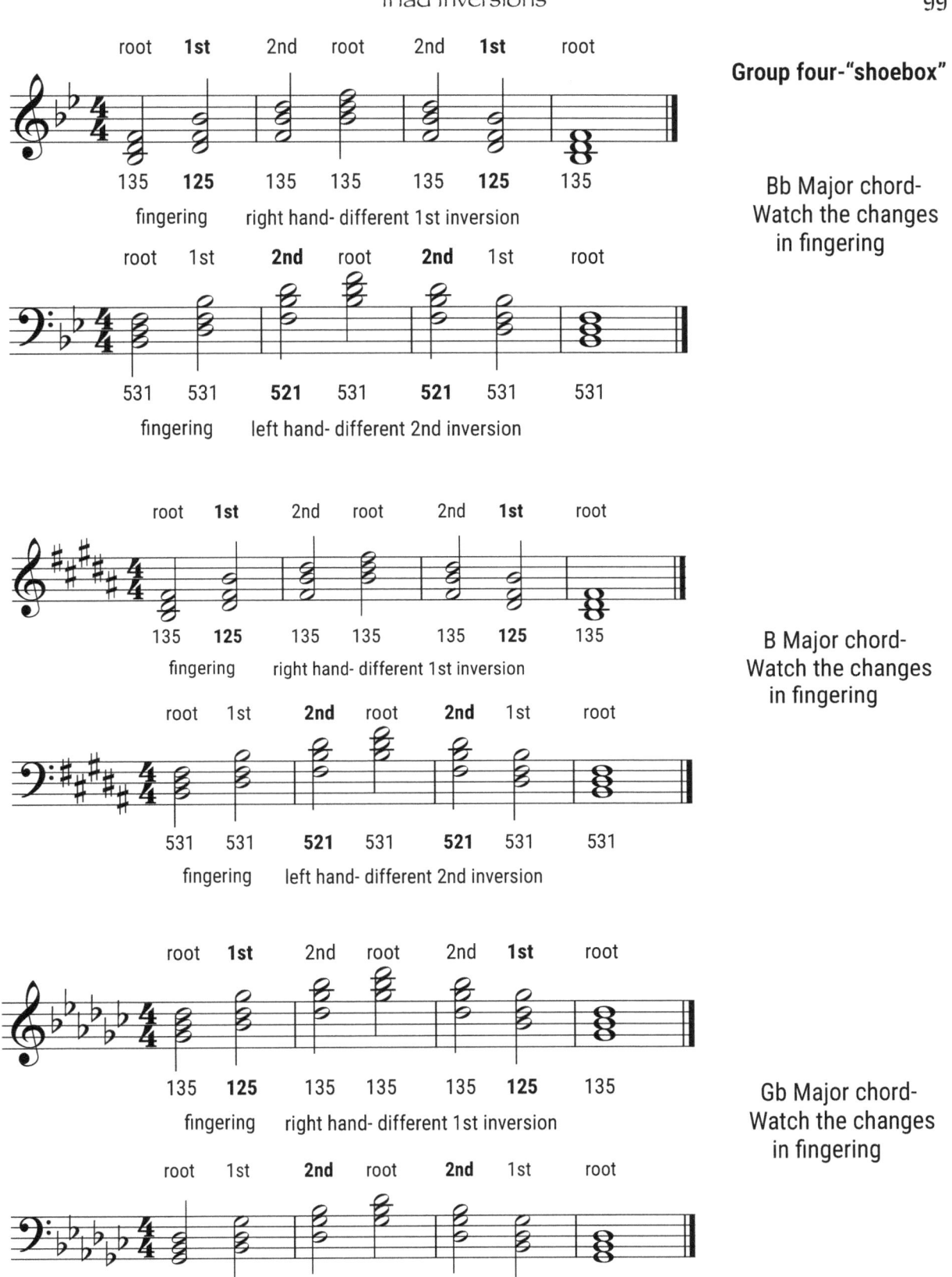

Group four-"shoebox"

Bb Major chord-
Watch the changes
in fingering

B Major chord-
Watch the changes
in fingering

Gb Major chord-
Watch the changes
in fingering

Triad Inversions

Hands Together

There are a few things to consider when playing these triads with the hands together.

The fingering changes in different places for each hand. But it's the same fingering for both hands when they both play the chord in root position. Learn the fingering pattern in both directions.

The fingering pattern is:
Same fingering for both hands in root position, **different RH** 1st inversion,
different LH 2nd inversion, then again **Same** fingering for both hands in root position.

Learn the pattern for the hands ascending and descending:

Same   different **Right**   different **Left**   Same   different **Left**   different **Right**   Same

Study the graphic below carefully. Then play the hands together ascending and descending.

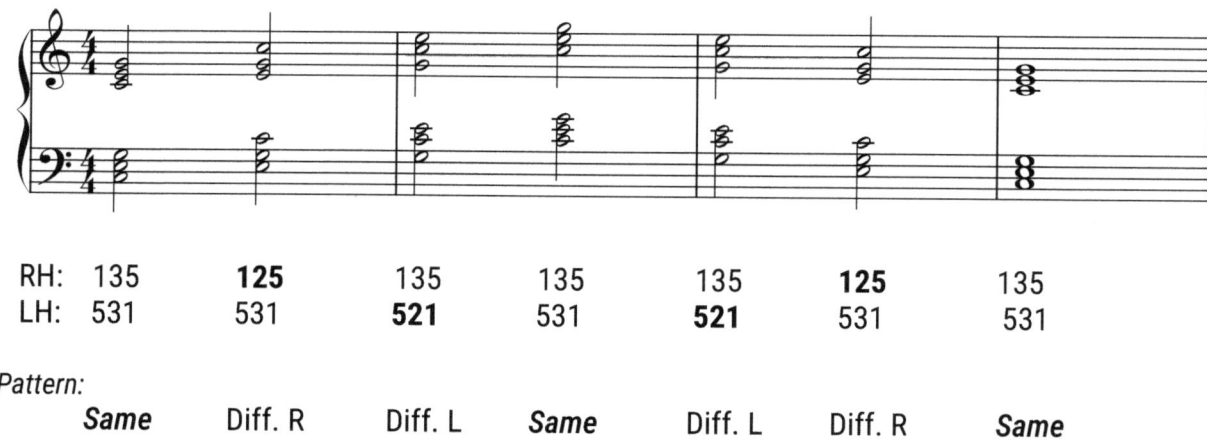

	Root position	1st inversion	2nd inversion	Root position	2nd inversion	1st inversion	Root position
RH:	135	**125**	135	135	135	**125**	135
LH:	531	531	**521**	531	**521**	531	531

Pattern:

	Same	Diff. R	Diff. L	*Same*	Diff. L	Diff. R	*Same*

Keep the hands relaxed and don't try to play it too fast at first. Gradually increase the speed.
Stay accurate with all the notes. Try to make them all equal in sound. Every note should sound at the exact same volume. If not, slow it down. Slow is good. Speed comes from accuracy..
Only go as fast as you can play these chords perfectly with the hands together using this fingering.

Triad Inversions

Using the 4 Groups– Major

It's much easier to learn all of the triads and inversions by dividing them into the 4 groups. We'll learn 3 *tonic I chords* in 3 keys at the same time. Begin with the first group, White/White/White. There are fingering changes for each hand. Keep this exact same fingering for all 12 keys.

It may seem easier with this first group to play of all these combinations with the same 135 531 fingering for all chords and inversions but it won't work in some other keys, like B. It's important at this stage to make as few changes as possible to learn all of them together. Changing fingering between keys creates more possibilities which can exponentially add more confusion. Later on you will use any fingering you like. But for now keep it simple to learn all of them at once. Memorize this fingering pattern. *Same, different right, different left, same, different left, different right, same.* Look carefully at this example in C. Then play all 12 keys with this exact same fingering pattern. First play the hands separately and then together. Make sure all of the notes sound equal.

First play the hands separately and then together. Make sure all the notes sound equal. Continue using the exact same fingerings- shown here for the first system on each page.

W/B/W

D

A

E

B/W/B

Eb

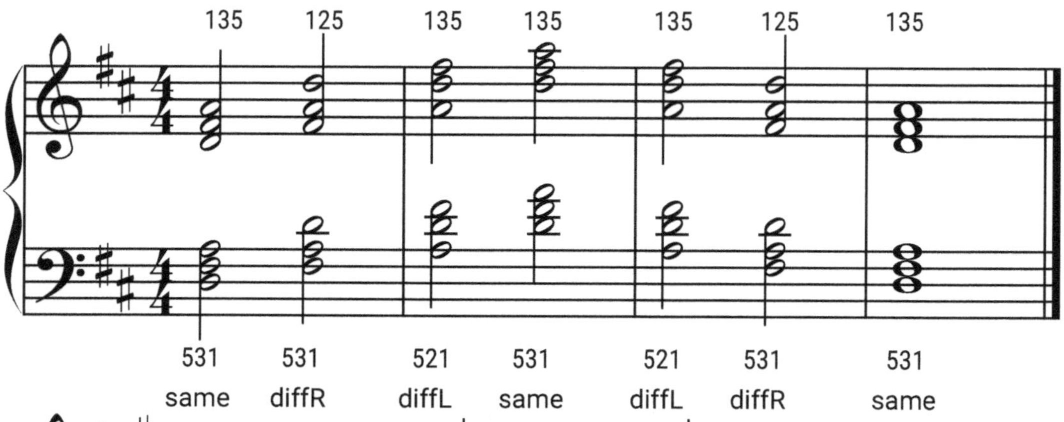

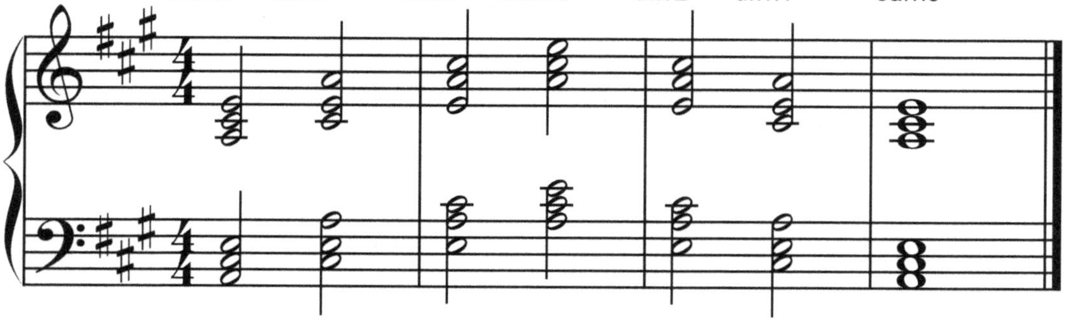

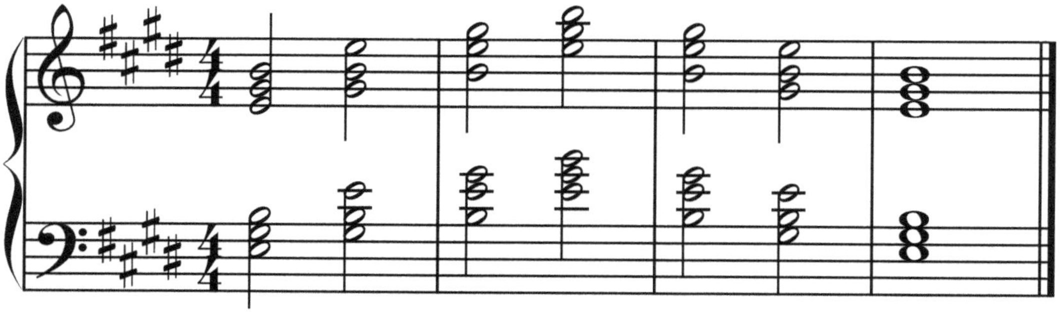

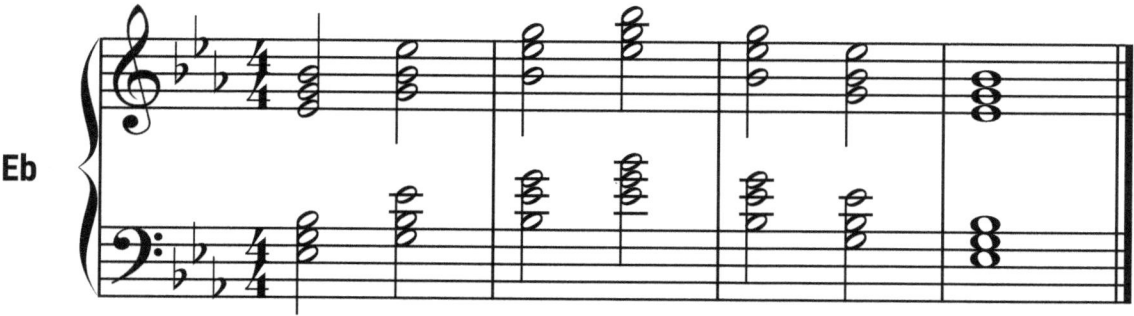

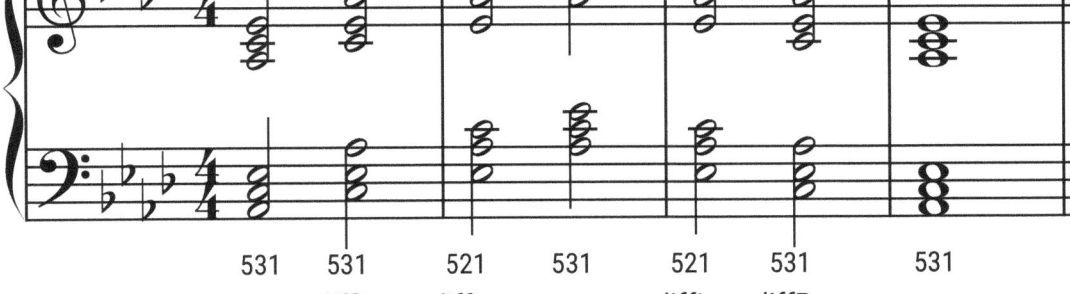

Ab

Db

'Shoebox'

Bb

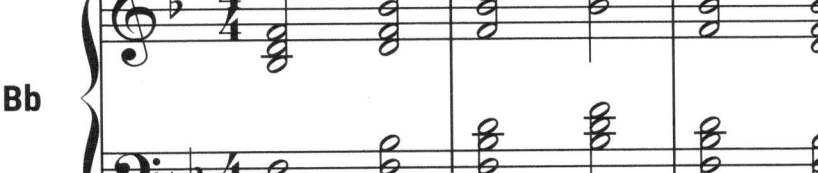

B

F#(Gb)

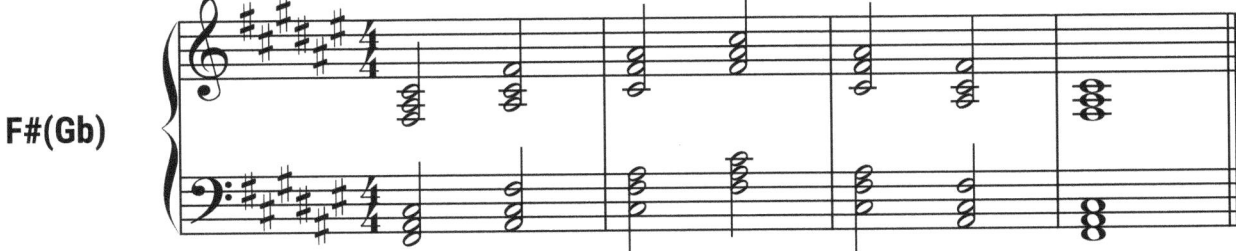

Minor Triad Inversions- hands together

Here we'll put all of the things together that we have just been working on and change just one element. This is something that occurs in musical situations often. Sometimes we only need to control one small bit of the entire expression. Here the 3rd is flatted by a half step to make it minor. Everything else is the same as you have just played, except here we will go through the keys using the two whole tone scale patterns in quarter notes. The two whole tone scales have six notes each.

Whole tone scale #1- C, D, E, F#, Ab, Bb

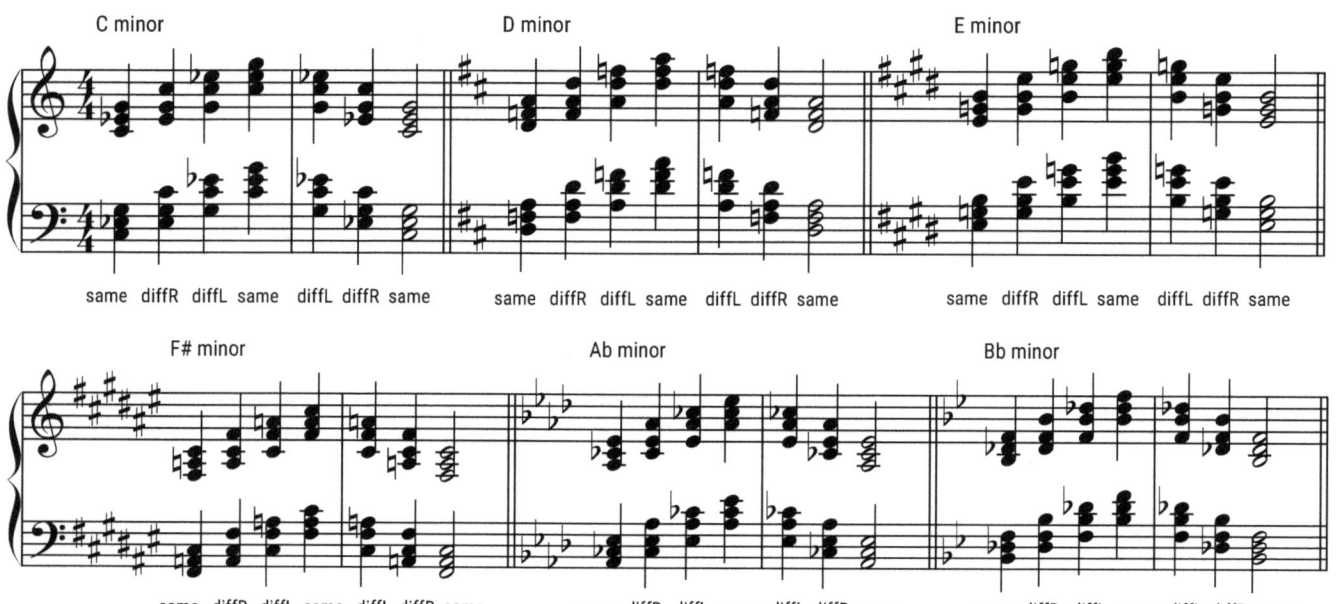

Whole tone scale #2: B, Db, Eb, F, G, A

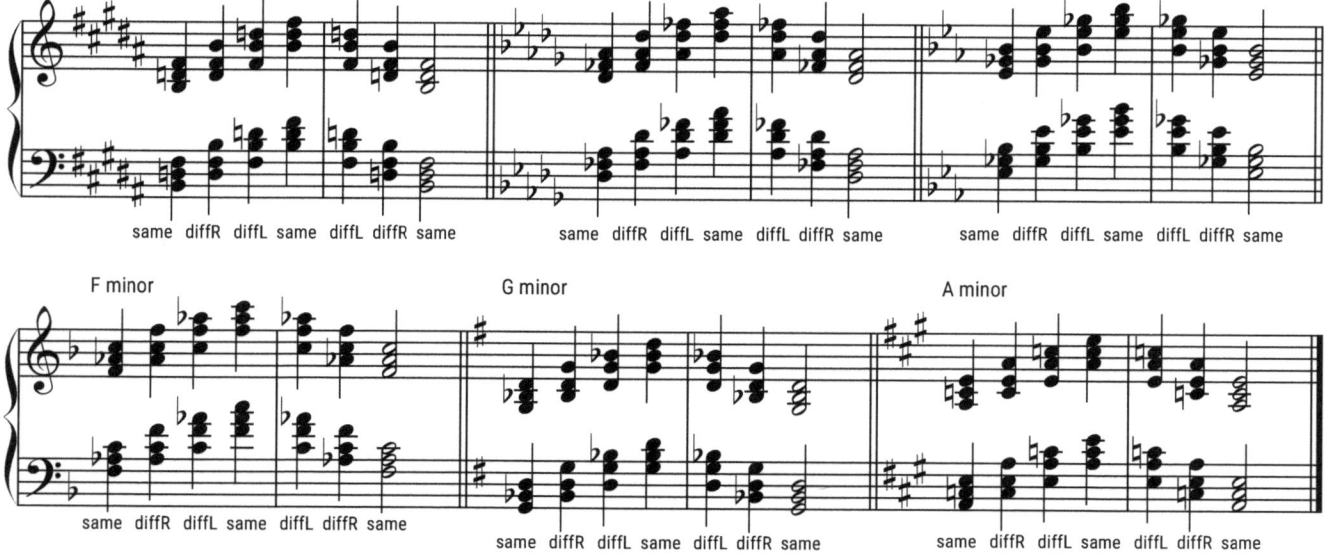

Whole Tone and Diminished Triad Inversions

When played together the twelve augmented triads and inversions can be divided into four groups of three "+" chords each. The symmetrical structure shows that they are all composed of two major 3rd intervals. We will soon see this chord divides the octave into three equal **major 3rd** sections.

Now play the two whole tone scales over the four different groups of augmented triads.

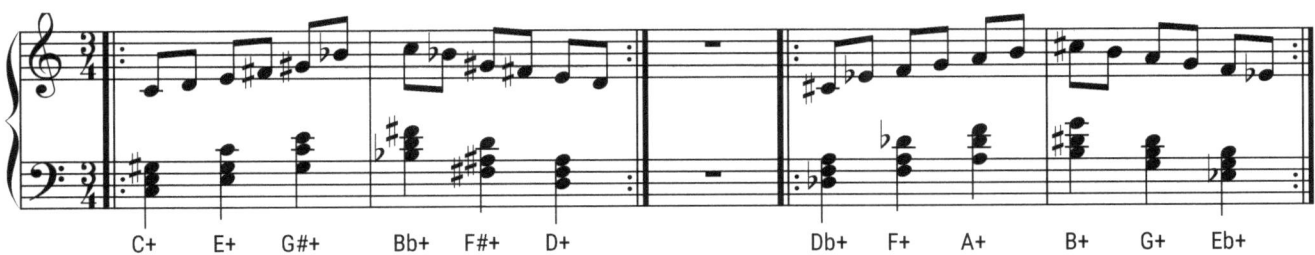

The 12 diminished triads can be combined into three groups of four chords each,. The symmetrical structure reveals they are all composed of minor 3rd intervals and outline three *diminished seventh chords*. We will soon see the *dim 7th* exactly divides the octave into four equal **minor 3rd** sections.

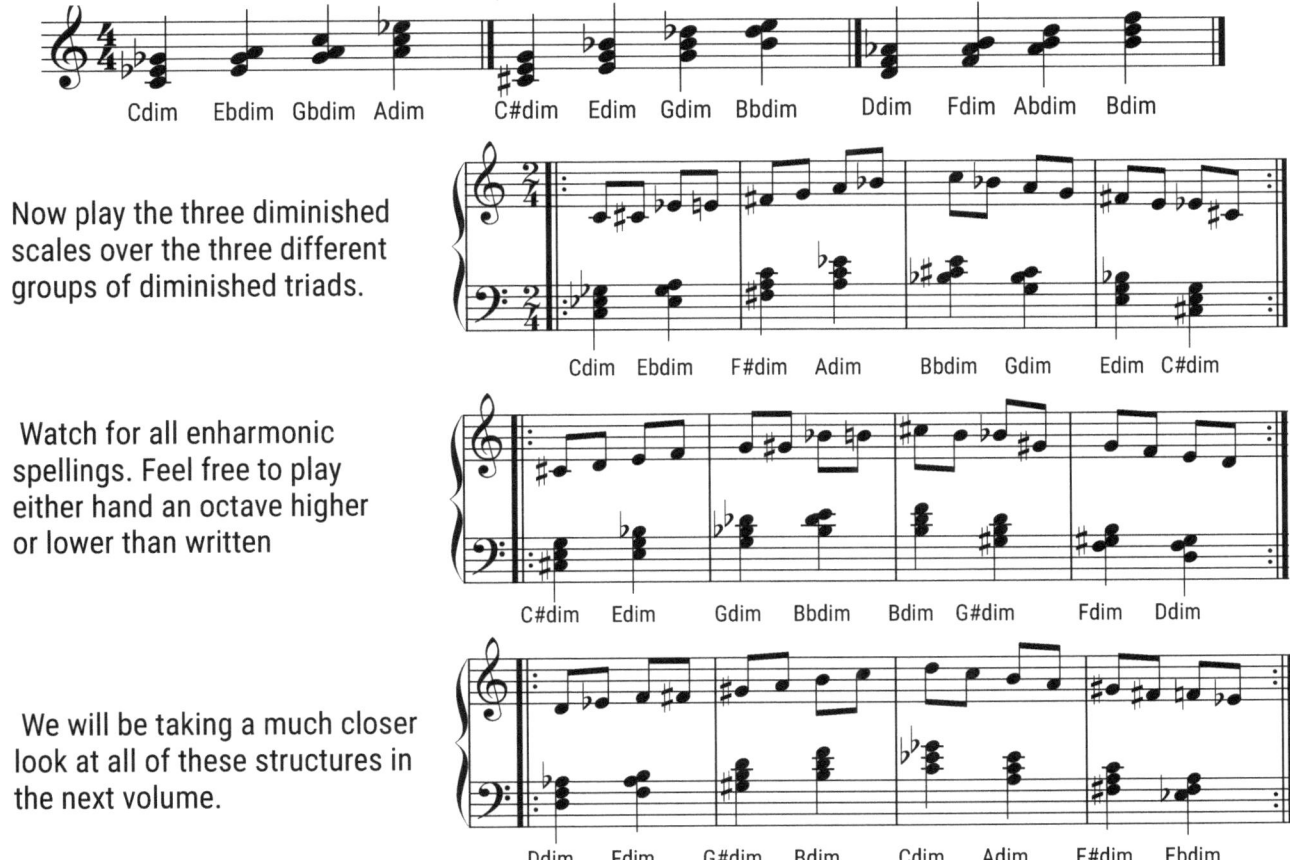

Now play the three diminished scales over the three different groups of diminished triads.

Watch for all enharmonic spellings. Feel free to play either hand an octave higher or lower than written

We will be taking a much closer look at all of these structures in the next volume.

Targeting Triads

After playing all of the major and minor triads and inversions in all the keys that knowledge has to be put to use in a practical form. Chords occur everywhere in musical situations, and the more skill you have with moving these shapes and harmonies the better. Once you are comfortable with these basic chords there is a great deal of music that becomes easier to play. That is because so much music is based on these harmonies in one form or another. You want to get to them quickly without hesitation. We have already targeted the root position triads through the circle over a left hand root pattern. The pattern is based on a counterclockwise movement on the circle going up a 4th and down a 5th. Right hand uses 135 fingering. Left hand uses 51 or 41 fingering.

When playing 1st inversion in the right hand use 125 fingering. Left hand uses 51 or 41 fingering.

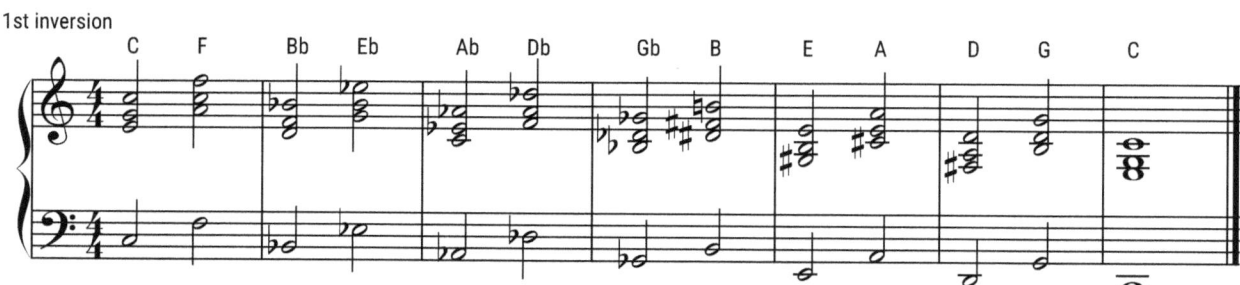

If the above is too hard or frustrating, start with the left hand a Major 3rd under the right hand instead of an octave lower and then it will be much easier. Play it as shown below. When it feels comfortable make sure to also then play the left hand as shown above. Keep 125 in the right hand and 51 or 41 in the left hand.

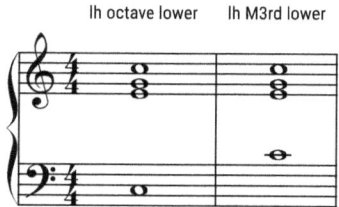

When playing 2nd inversion in the right hand use 531 fingering. Left hand uses 51 or 41.

Targeting minor triads

Now play root position **minor** triads by flatting the 3rd of the chord. 135 rh and 51 or 41 lh.

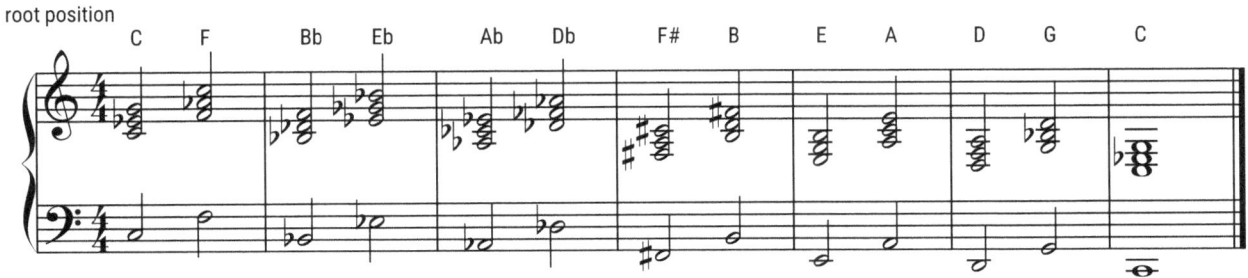

When playing 1st inversion in the right hand use 125 fingering. Left hand uses 51 or 41 fingering. Again if this is a little hard try playing this inversion with the left hand closer like you did on the previous page but using a **minor 3rd** under the right hand. Then play as shown an octave lower.

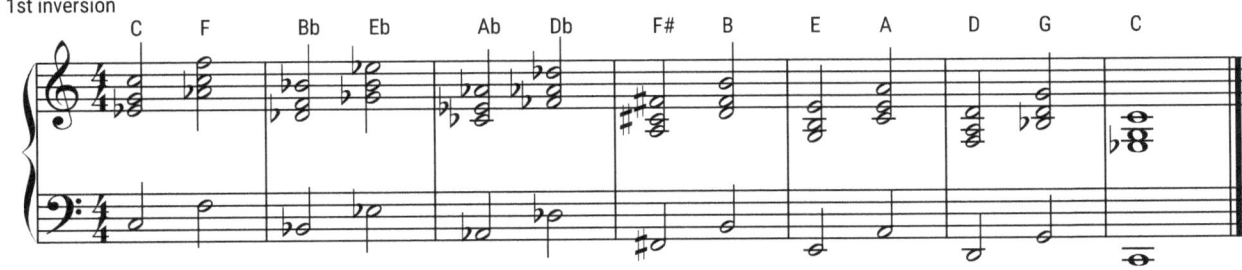

When playing 2nd inversion in the right hand use 135 fingering. Left hand uses 51 or 41.

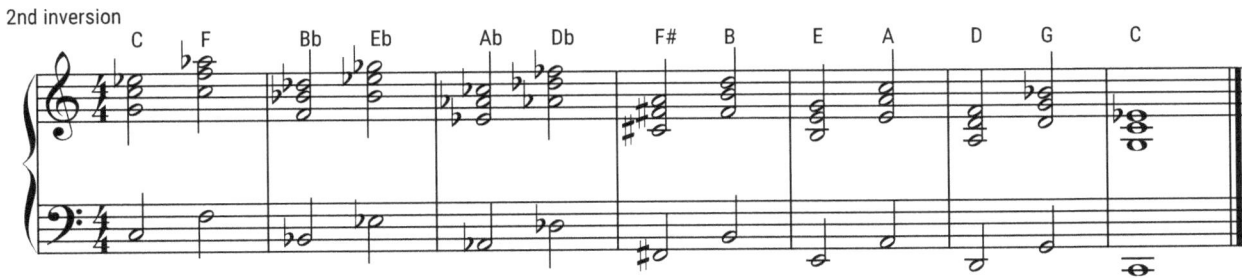

Targeting Triads

Hands Together- Major

The Major and minor triads are the building blocks of much of the music we encounter. As a player you will benefit greatly by having these shapes under your fingers. As harmonies they are used constantly in their basic form or in more complex extended harmonies like rootless voicings or as upper structures. It's important to spend enough time playing and absorbing these shapes so they become relaxed and natural in your thinking and your hands, almost automatic. We want the connection between the mind and the hands to be so solid and our abilities to be so fluid that as the mind thinks of a chord the hand is already there. The final step in this part of our study of triads and inversions will be playing triads with both hands moving together in parallel motion.

Major triad in root position- counterclockwise through the circle of 5ths. Use 135 rh and 531 lh.

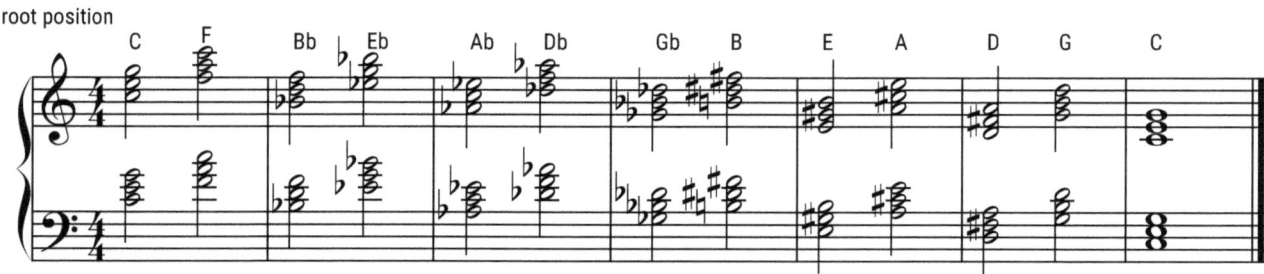

Major triad in 1st inversion- counterclockwise through the circle of 5ths. Use **125 rh** and 531 lh.

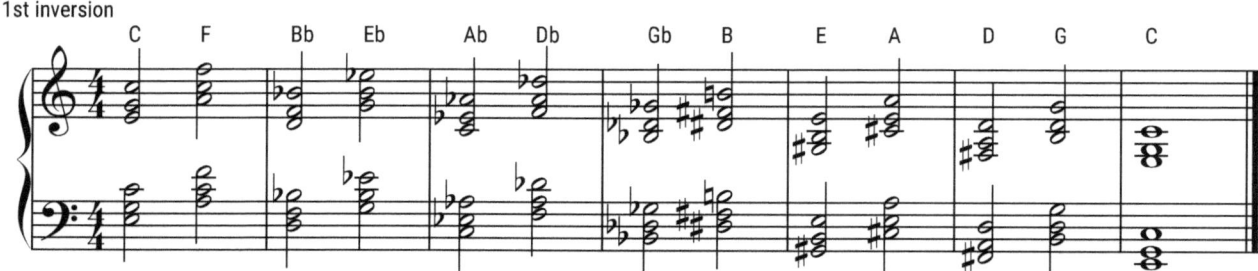

Major triad in 2nd inversion- counterclockwise through the circle of 5ths. Use 135 rh and **521 lh**.

Hands Together- minor

Hopefully by now the chords are becoming more familiar. Here again we flat the third of each chord to change it from Major to minor. The hands move in parallel motion through the circle. It might actually start becoming faster now as you continue playing through these patterns and get used to them. The hands can help each other by moving together through all the shapes at the same time. Trust the process. Also learning the circle of 5ths at the same time will prove to be of even more value as we begin to play music with V I, II V I, or VI II V I root movements or chord progressions. Playing counterclockwise on the circle of 5ths follows those same patterns so we are playing them in an order that is used in music constantly. Root movements or chord sequences using V I or II V I progressions are used in almost every style of music. Not only are 4ths and 5ths strong intervals- *perfect*- but harmonies often connect to each other by root movements and progressions using the interval of a 4th or 5th.

Minor triad in root position- counterclockwise through the circle of 5ths. Use 135 rh and 531 lh.

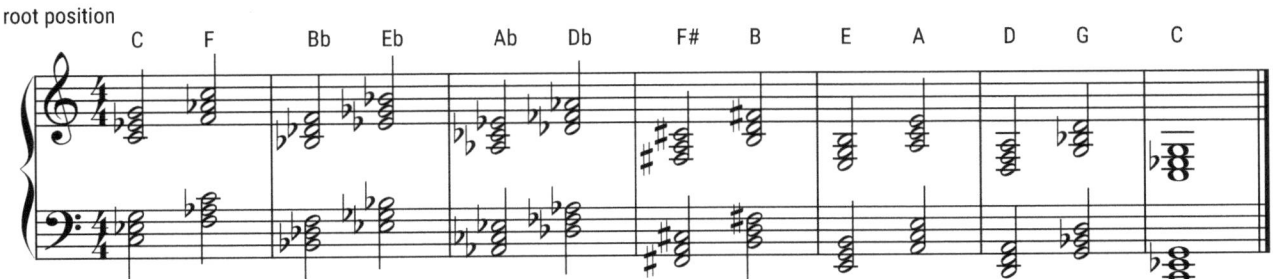

Minor triad in 1st inversion- counterclockwise through the circle of 5ths. Use **125 rh** and 531 lh.

Minor triad in 2nd inversion- counterclockwise through the circle of 5ths. Use 135 rh and **521 lh**.

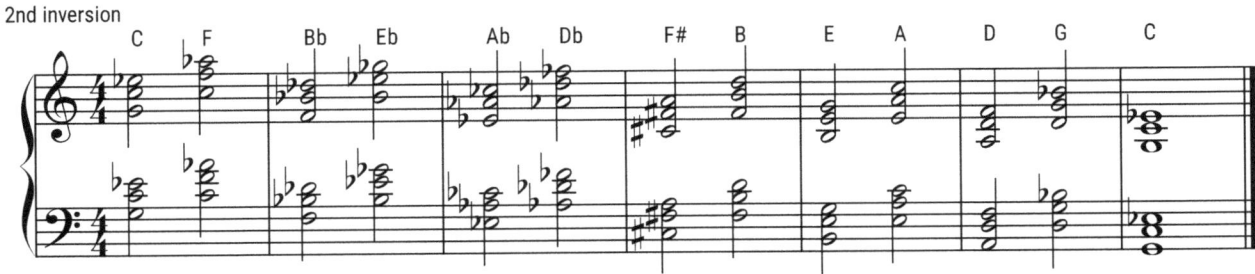

Learn to change just one part of a pattern without changing the rest, a good skill to perfect.
Play these examples from pages 106-109 but with the pattern reversed- down a 5th, up a 4th.
First play the major chord over the root. Remember 521 for 1st inversion in the right hand.

Then play the major chords with the hands together- 125 rh in 1st inversion, 521 lh in 2nd inversion.

Now play the minor triad over the root. Remember 125 for 1st inversion in the right hand.

Then play the minor triads with the hands together. 125 rh in 1st inversion, 521 lh in 2nd inversion.

Major Scale Patterns on the Keyboard
Patterns for Sharp Keys

The black and white keys form patterns on the piano keyboard for every key. Each key has it's own distinctive pattern that can be felt and seen. The black keys have a unique configuration for each of the sharp and flat keys. It can be helpful to imagine these patterns when playing the major scales.

Black key patterns for the sharp keys.

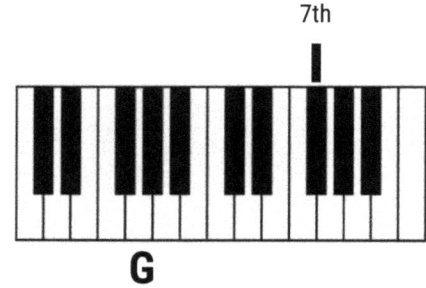

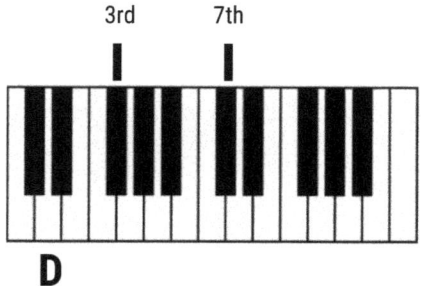

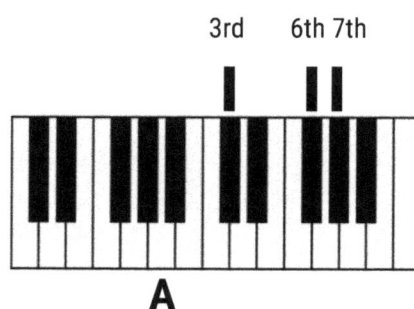

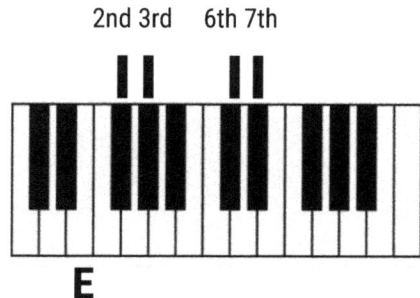

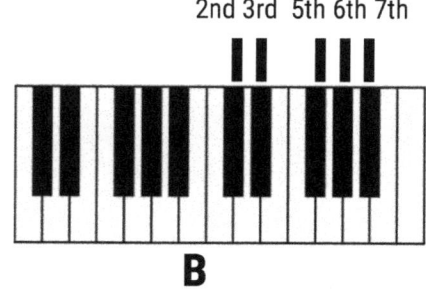

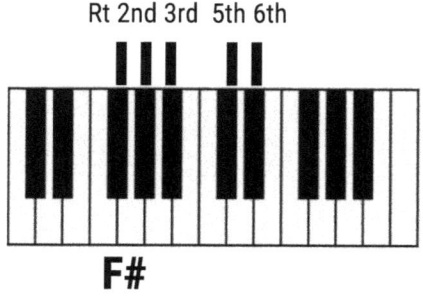

Try to see the individual pattern for each key. As we look at the flat keys there will be several keys that reverse the black and white key pattern from the sharp keys.

Major Scale Patterns on the Keyboard
Patterns for Flat Keys

Here are the black key patterns for the flat keys. There are patterns that **exactly reverse** some of the black and white key patterns from the sharp keys. Allow these to help you organize the keys.

Bb has 2 **black** keys on the root and 4th. B has 2 **white** keys on the root and 4th, a color reversal. Eb, Ab, and Db are similar color reversals of E, A, and D respectively.

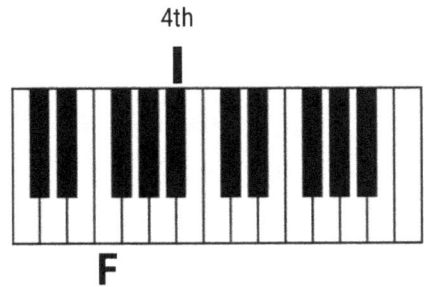

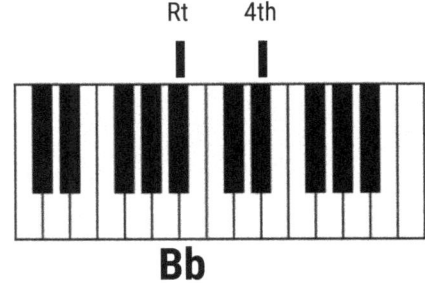

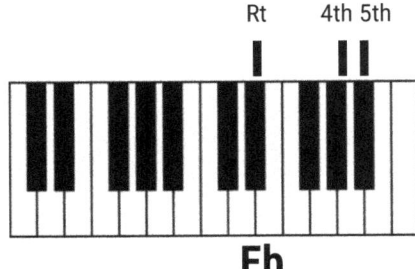

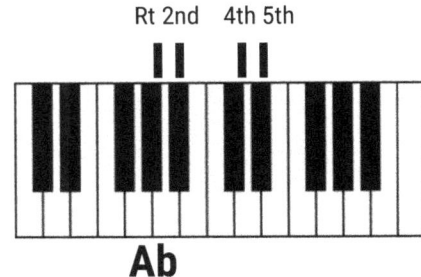

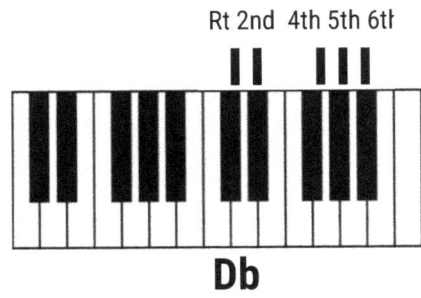

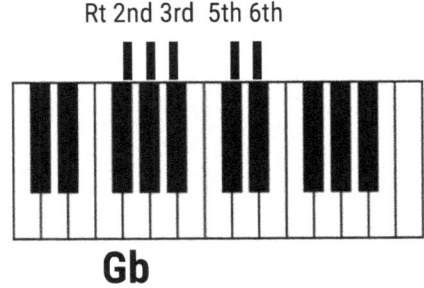

These black key patterns are unique for each key. As you assimilate them they will help you to identify each scale and it's own particular shape, enabling more confident movement between the keys. They will become real friends. Take your time and absorb them at a relaxed pace.

Broken Chords in C Major

There are six basic broken chord patterns. They are shown here in C major written in their entirety. There are two different combinations for each finger that begins a broken chord pattern. The first and easiest of these starts with the root. Since we tend to reverse this pattern when reversing direction (i.e. root-3rd-5th-3rd ascending becomes 5th-3rd-root-3rd descending) carefully watch that it is the exact same pattern for both ascending **and** descending. We are trying to be fluid with any playing situation and these lesser played combinations often turn out to be quite musical. The idea here is to try reversing our usual programming and create new ways to hear and think. This will be even more valuable a skillset as we incorporate elements of rhythm. So it is very important here to play **all** of the permutations carefully as written so we don't face those obstacles later on.

First combination starting with the root. Roman numerals are shown for the first pattern.
Use 135 fingers in the right hand and 531 in the left for all chords.

Root--3rd-5th-3rd

Root-5th-3rd-5th

The second set of patterns begins with the 3rd of the chord played by the 3rd finger in both hands. This is actually somewhat difficult because we have to move the entire hand into position first before we play a note. Try to visualize the I-VII triads of the major scale and the qualities of each as you move. Strive for an even sound for all the notes. Memorize the qualities of the chords.

I, IV, and V are major
ii, iii, and vi are minor
vii is diminished.

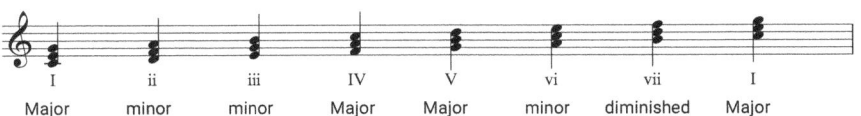

Second combination starting with the 3rd.

3rd-root-3rd-5th

3rd-5th-3rd-root

The third combination starts on the 5th of the chord. Visualize the I-VII pattern while moving up and down through the key. All of the notes should sound equal in volume and duration.

Third combination starting with the 5th.
Use 135 fingers in the right hand and 531 in the left for all chords.

5th-3rd-root-3rd

5th-root-3rd-root

Only the ascending measures of these six combinations will be shown for the rest of the keys. Use the keyboard graphic to help you see and feel the unique shape of each key on the keyboard. Along the way you may play different notes that sound good to you but make sure to play the familiar I-VII pattern in every key. Refer to pages 56-58 as needed to help with understanding these chords and patterns for each key.

Play the exact same pattern ascending and then **descending**.

Root-3rd-5th-3rd

Root-5th-3rd-5th

3rd-root-3rd-5th

3rd-5th-3rd-root

5th-3rd-root-3rd

5th-root-3rd-root

Play the exact same pattern ascending and then **descending**.

Root--3rd-5th-3rd

Root-5th-3rd-5th

3rd-root-3rd-5th

3rd-5th-3rd-root

5th-3rd-root-3rd

5th-root-3rd-root

Broken Chords- A Major

Play the exact same pattern ascending and then **descending.**

Root--3rd-5th-3rd

Root-5th-3rd-5th

3rd-root-3rd-5th

3rd-5th-3rd-root

5th-3rd-root-3rd

5th-root-3rd-root

Broken Chords- E Major

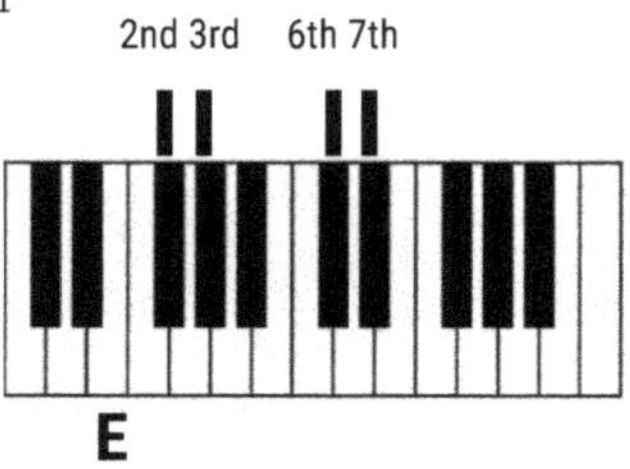

Play the exact same pattern ascending and descending.

Root--3rd-5th-3rd

Root-5th-3rd-5th

3rd-root-3rd-5th

3rd-5th-3rd-root

5th-3rd-root-3rd

5th-root-3rd-root

Broken Chords- B Major

Play the exact same pattern ascending and **descending**.

Root--3rd-5th-3rd

Root-5th-3rd-5th

3rd-root-3rd-5th

3rd-5th-3rd-root

5th-3rd-root-3rd

5th-root-3rd-root

Broken Chords- F Major

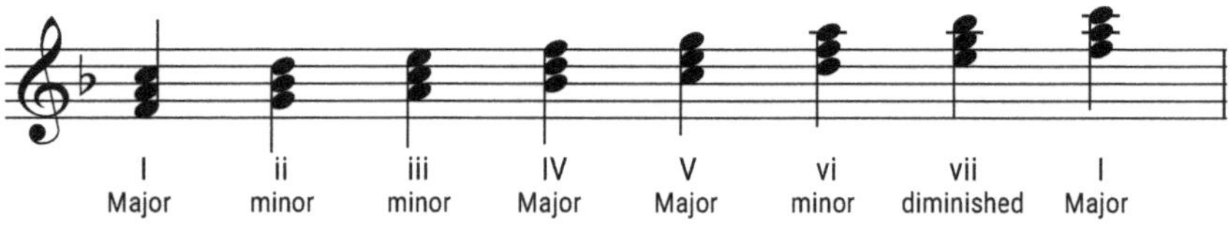

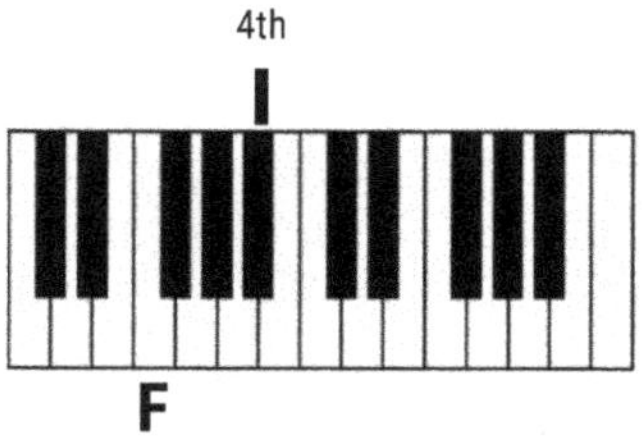

I	ii	iii	IV	V	vi	vii	I
Major	minor	minor	Major	Major	minor	diminished	Major

4th

F

Play the exact same pattern ascending and descending.

Root--3rd-5th-3rd

Root-5th-3rd-5th

3rd-root-3rd-5th

3rd-5th-3rd-root

5th-3rd-root-3rd

5th-root-3rd-root

Chapter 5- Triads and Inversions

Play the exact same pattern ascending and **descending**.

Root--3rd-5th-3rd

Root-5th-3rd-5th

3rd-root-3rd-5th

3rd-5th-3rd-root

5th-3rd-root-3rd

5th-root-3rd-root

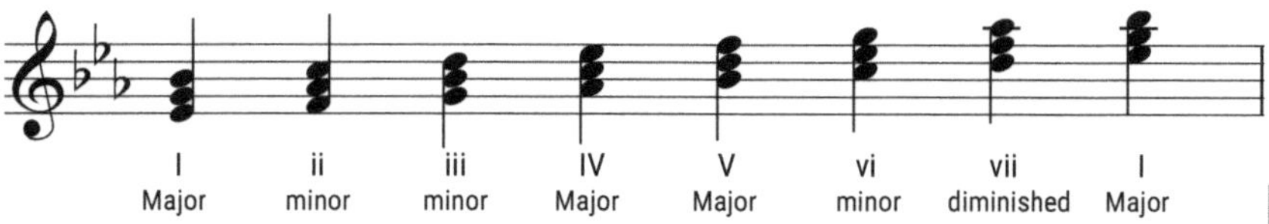

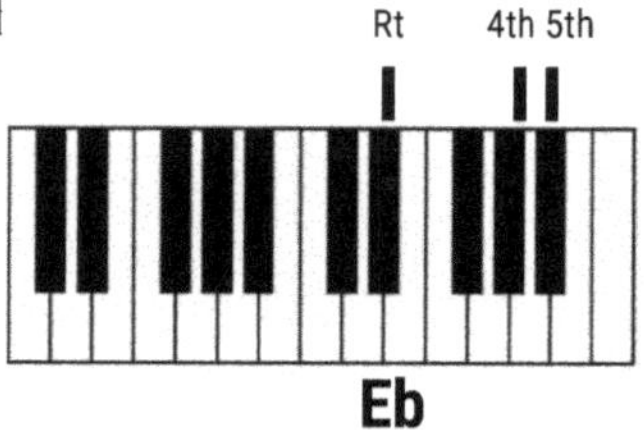

I   ii   iii   IV   V   vi   vii   I
Major   minor   minor   Major   Major   minor   diminished   Major

Rt   4th   5th

Eb

Play the exact same pattern ascending and descending.

Root–3rd-5th-3rd

Root-5th-3rd-5th

3rd-root-3rd-5th

3rd-5th-3rd-root

5th-3rd-root-3rd

5th-root-3rd-root

Play the exact same pattern ascending and **descending**.

Root--3rd-5th-3rd

Root-5th-3rd-5th

3rd-root-3rd-5th

3rd-5th-3rd-root

5th-3rd-root-3rd

5th-root-3rd-root

I   ii   iii   IV   V   vi   vii   I

Major   minor   minor   Major   Major   minor   diminished   Major

Rt 2nd 4th 5th 6th

Db

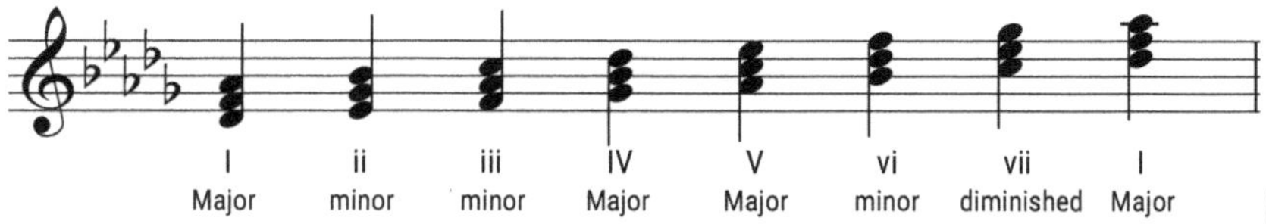

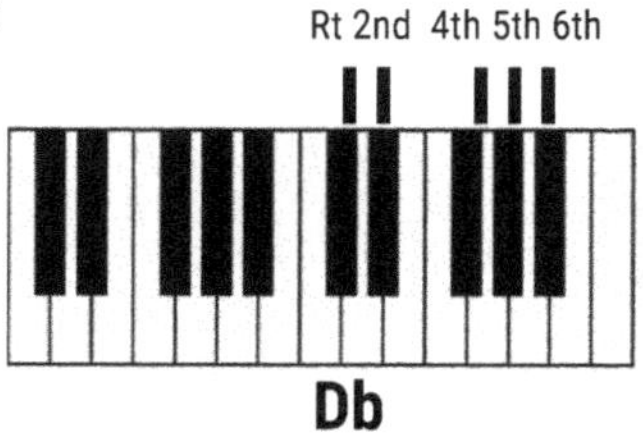

Play the exact same pattern ascending and **descending**.

Root--3rd-5th-3rd

Root-5th-3rd-5th

3rd-root-3rd-5th

3rd-5th-3rd-root

5th-3rd-root-3rd

5th-root-3rd-root

Broken Chords- Gb(F#) Major

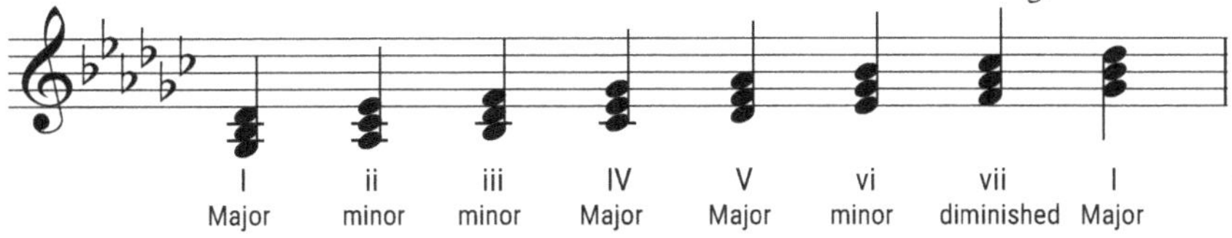

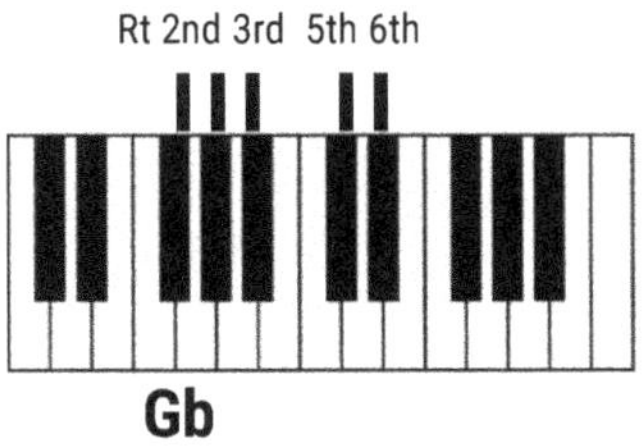

I	ii	iii	IV	V	vi	vii	I
Major	minor	minor	Major	Major	minor	diminished	Major

Rt 2nd 3rd 5th 6th

Gb

Play the exact same pattern ascending and descending.

Root–3rd-5th-3rd

Root-5th-3rd-5th

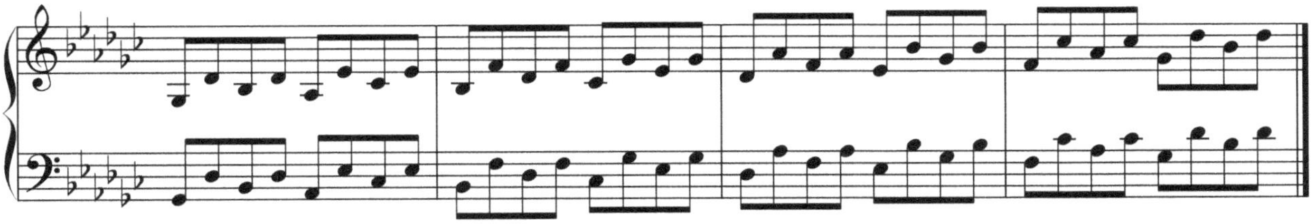

3rd-root-3rd-5th

3rd-5th-3rd-root

5th-3rd-root-3rd

5th-root-3rd-root

Now play all of the broken chord combinations using the *1st inversion*. Remember 125 rh.
Play the exact same patterns ascending and **descending** in C, and then play them in the other keys.

3rd-5th-Root-5th

3rd-Root-5th-Root

5th-3rd-5th-Root

5th-Root-5th-3rd

Root-5th-3rd-5th

Root-3rd-5th-3rd

Then play all of the broken chord combinations using the *2nd inversion*. Remember 521 lh.
Play the exact same patterns ascending and **descending** in C, and then play them in the other keys.

5th-Root-3rd-Root

5th-3rd-Root-3rd

Root-5th-Root-3rd

Root-3rd-Root-5th

3rd-Root-5th-Root

3rd-5th-Root-5th

Try adding an octave to **any** of the basic triads or inversions. Some of these are difficult to play because of the large stretches so don't over extend your hand if it's too hard. Play them as broken chords. Listen to how the octave changes and strengthens the sounds of the different shapes.

As you play these octave patterns over time you may notice that the fingertips will get closer to the keys and use just the small 'zone' at the lower area of the black keys that bridges the white keys. The hands will eventually require very little energy and motion between the different colors. As your fingers become familiar with both the black and white keys you will find that all 12 scales get easier under the hands. We'll start this process playing the chromatic scale in octaves with the hands separately and then together ascending and descending. Use the **4th finger for all black keys** and the 5th finger for all white keys. The right hand uses 15 and 14 fingering.

Then play octaves in the left hand using 51 fingering for the white keys and 41 for the black keys.

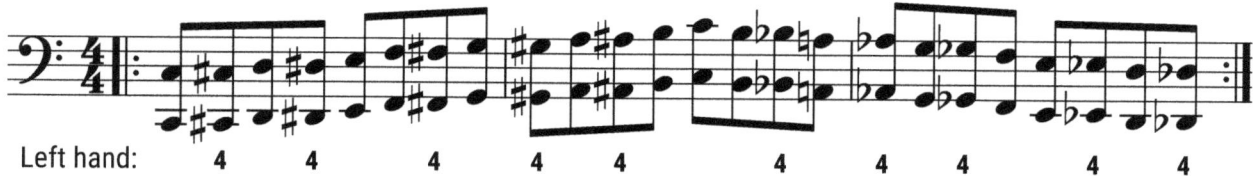

Now play the hands together in parallel motion using the same fingerings.

When this feels comfortable go ahead and play two or more octaves ascending and descending. You might also try the hands playing in contrary motion as a more challenging way to play these. Make sure to then play the triads and inversions with added octaves in some other keys.

If you play an octave on any note it could potentially be one of three notes in a triad: The root, 3rd, or 5th. There are 4 basic triads. Play an octave on the note F and then play the following chords. F is a member of three major and three minor triads played as the root, 3rd, or 5th of that chord.

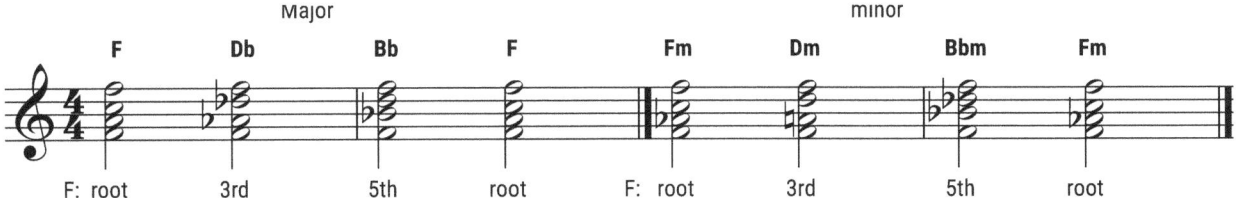

The great ragtime composer Scott Joplin used this idea extensively in his music with an innovative approach by playing an octave with an added 3rd interval in the left hand as a chord voicing. Look at this idea with an octave on C and adding a major or minor 3rd within the octave, lower or higher.

See how many basic triads you can spell using C played as an octave with an added 3rd.

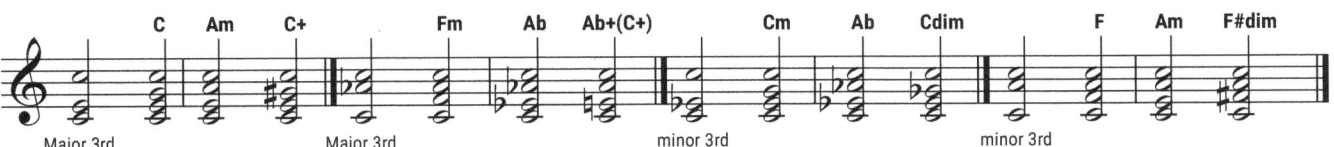

Here is a left hand chord progression played in a stride piano style. First play the chord pattern as triads with an added octave. Then play the chords broken up differently using 10th intervals. A 10th can be thought of as a major or minor 3rd above the octave. This is a much more interesting way to play various chords in the left hand and is used quite a bit in certain styles of music from many different eras, including the baroque era.

This is a big stretch for the left hand so if you find it too hard play these shapes as broken chords.

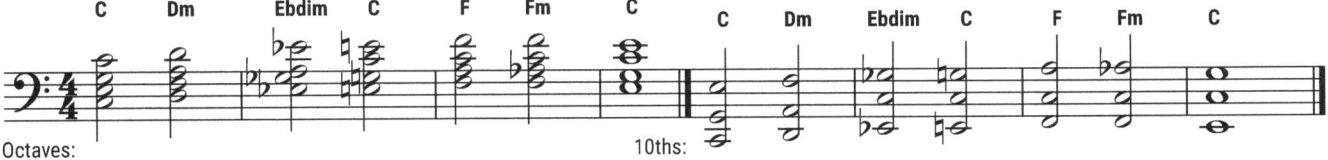

Throughout this study we've examined chords and scales as structures and how even the most basic shapes combine in many permutations and variations. As you assimilate the fundamental language presented to this point it would be helpful, and hopefully very satisfying, to see these principles used in actual music. The following pages present a few musical examples that will serve as both a summary of the information presented so far and proof that it is being absorbed.

Summary Compositions

Compositions using Scales and Chords

A knowledge of basic scales and chords helps us play an abundance of music from so many different styles and different musical minds. Here is an example from Leopold Mozart's *Nannerl Notenbuch*, a series of pieces given to his daughter (and Wolfgang's older sister). Leopold was a well respected composer and gave books of music to both of his children, presented to each of them at an early age to help with their musical studies.

Here is a pretty song that outlines both major and minor harmonies by using scales- shown with minimal fingering. Try to figure out the outlines of the harmonies, basic chords, and hand positions. Start slowly with the hands separately and then together listening to these different sounds.
This is also a good study to learn about musical form. As you can see, there are two 8 measure systems that each have a repeat sign. The first system could be considered the "A" section of the song and the second system the "B" section. Playing each section twice as indicated would be called AABB form. Try playing the second system only once, or AAB. Play around with the form.
Count the *triplet* in measure 15 by saying the syllables tri-pa-let equally for one beat (quarter note).

Here is a selection from the **Note Book for Wolfgang,** one of several books presented to each of
Leopold Mozart's two children. The elder Mozart was a well known composer in his own right.
These delightful books contain both original pieces and collected songs that were intended to
teach music to Wolfgang and his older sister. Young Wolfgang soon began writing his own original
compositions and then notating them on some of the blank pages his father had left in the books.

This wonderful song is in a stately dance form known as a **Polonaise**, typically in 3/4.
Try to see this piece as mostly outlining basic triads and shapes from the C major scale.
Play the hands separately and then together as you get comfortable playing the entire song.
Only minimal fingering is shown to encourage you to see the familiar structures and positions.
The right hand outlines I or vii chords and their inversions, adding octaves in measures 11-12.
The left hand plays octaves on the I, IV, or V (C, F, and G) of the C scale, using a low- high pattern
except for the last measure of each **8 bar system**, where you play the final two notes as high-low.

Repeat signs are open to interpretation, allowing the song to be played in several different forms.

The *Minuet in G* by Johann Sebastian Bach is a short piece intended to outline and teach the basic shapes one encounters when moving around in that key and it's neighboring harmonies. Today's music still has many similarities in the use of these shapes and how they relate to each other. At times the piece can sound quite modern for this reason. So consider Bach's study to be a timeless master class in it's relevance. First it is presented without any fingering to allow you to develop your own way of seeing the familiar shapes and the chords and scales used. Then the facing page shows some minimal suggested fingering to help you to develop an approach using these shapes. Feel free to experiment with your own fingering, but chances are you will end up using this basic suggested fingering. Play the hands separately at first and listen carefully to each part, especially to the melodic part in the left hand that accompanies the main melody played in the right hand.

Now play it using our understanding of these outlines as they start to feel natural under the hands.
The key signature of G major is shown, so remember to play F# when you see an F in the score.
As you become more acquainted with the shapes and movements feel free to change any fingering
if it's easier. However be warned: write all fingering in *pencil only*, as often you will change it later.

The small *grace note* (B) in measure eight should be played as a very short *ornament* that leads to
the downbeat (A). Typically ornaments from the Baroque period also have other approaches and
you may see them notated in several variants suggesting the many different ways that they can be
played. Music is a living language and is constantly being informed by various interpretations.

Congratulations! By making it through this first volume a fascinating process is already at work organizing for you. The patterns in our musical world are taking shape within your imagination and hopefully you are gaining a good comprehension of them. As you continue on your musical journey that understanding will deepen. Just by playing the piano and moving your fingers you are building these neural pathways. The connections are reinforced the more you play, so enjoy the process.

The point of this study is to help you organize all of these patterns in your own way organically. The patterns themselves already exist within the musical world. Since there are far too many of them to understand all at once- or fit into any one book- let your mind absorb and prioritize things at it's own speed as you build a stronger foundation. The goal is to build this foundation in your subconscious mind as it becomes activated in a way that will likely seem almost mysterious.

You may begin to have a sense of your musical understanding clearing up as if by magic, without spending long hours mindlessly playing scales and exercises. Playing without fully using all of your brainpower is truly a waste of time. And why miss out on all the fun? Your mind loves working on a higher level and music does this automatically. Push yourself into new territory and discoveries.

Here we cultivate the exact opposite of mindless: *mindfulness*. And most importantly, heart.

The great Maurice Ravel believed that music without feeling isn't worth the paper it's written on.

Of course you will still have to do some work to get anywhere, but never lose your focus and full awareness. A good rule of thumb is to pick different things to challenge yourself. Stay engaged. Always listen carefully and practice **that** too. Your ears are the most important instrument.

Because this system is based on how to think about music, it is important to understand how much that process continues everywhere we look around us. Beethoven himself is said to have used bird songs in his *Pastorale* Symphony. Make it a part of your daily life to enjoy music and then to try to identify what it is that you like about it. See if there are any particular chords, scales, or patterns you can recognize. Listen to your favorites and let your imagination work through the musical passages that engage your mind and develop your curiosity. Nothing is required of you but to continue letting this process work naturally. You will only get better at it as long as you keep going and continue listening to the infinite number of musical worlds that await your exploring.

It is my sincere hope that you have enjoyed this book and that it has helped to open some doors to creativity and the many possibilities ahead for you.

Are You Ready To Continue Your Musical Adventures?
Be Sure To Check Out The Next Book In This Series:

The Musical Gift- volume two: Exploring Harmony

www.ingramcontent.com/pod-product-compliance
Lightning Source LLC
Chambersburg PA
CBHW041537120626
46551CB00019B/2725